ELEME

HARMONY

PART I

BY

C. H. KITSON

M.A. Cantab., D.Mus. Oxon.

PROFESSOR OF MUSIC IN THE UNIVERSITY OF DUBLIN

OXFORD   NEW YORK
OXFORD UNIVERSITY PRESS

Oxford University Press, Walton Street, Oxford OX2 6DP

Oxford New York Toronto
Delhi Bombay Calcutta Madras Karachi
Petaling Jaya Singapore Hong Kong Tokyo
Nairobi Dar es Salaam Cape Town
Melbourne Auckland

and associated companies in
Berlin Ibadan

Oxford is a trade mark of Oxford University Press

First published 1920
Twenty-seventh impression 1990

Printed in Great Britain by
St Edmundsbury Press Limited
Bury St Edmunds, Suffolk

PREFACE

MY *Evolution of Harmony* was intended for students of some maturity, and for those who are able to devote a considerable time to the subject.

A large number of those who have used it have expressed a wish that I should write a short elementary treatise on similar lines. The present book is the first part of this work. It is intended for beginners, for use in schools, and for students in musical institutions who have to acquire in a short time a knowledge of the main facts of harmony. In attempting to make the book short and concise, I have been compelled to make it somewhat dogmatic. As the book is for beginners, this is probably an advantage. No attempt is made to deal with modern technique. Obviously such a course would be quite out of place in a book of this nature.

In the preparation of this volume I have kept in the foreground what I think are the essentials for any profitable study: (*a*) ear-training, (*b*) constructive work, (*c*) constant use of the unessential.

If the study of harmony is to be of any use at all, it must enable the student to use the material about which he reads, even if it be in the most elementary fashion.

C. H. KITSON.

CONTENTS

CONTENTS

CHAPTER I

EAR-TRAINING IN THE DIATONIC
MAJOR SCALE

1. THE student must never be allowed to put down on paper what he does not hear both physically and mentally. It is not possible to hear mentally without having first heard physically. This chapter deals with the necessary preliminary ear-training.

2. The major diatonic scale:

Ex. 1.
C major.

The Roman numerals are used to designate the various degrees of the scale. The ordinary names are as follows:

I. Tonic, II. Supertonic, III. Mediant, IV. Subdominant, V. Dominant, VI. Submediant *or* Superdominant, VII. Leading Note.

3.

I to II	forms the interval of a		major second.
I to III	„	„	major third.
I to IV	„	„	perfect fourth.
I to V	„	„	perfect fifth.
I to VI	„	„	major sixth.
I to VII	„	„	major seventh.
I to I¹ (octave)	„	„	perfect octave.

When the sounds forming the interval are played consecutively, the interval is said to be melodic; when they are played simultaneously, the interval is harmonic.

Ex. 2.
Melodic intervals from I:

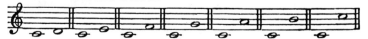

Harmonic intervals from I:

4. When intervals exceed the octave they are said to be compound.

The compound interval of the second is termed the ninth.

"	"	"	third	"	"	tenth.
"	"	"	fourth	"	"	eleventh.
"	"	"	fifth	"	"	twelfth.
"	"	"	sixth	"	"	thirteenth.
"	"	"	seventh	"	"	fourteenth.

But the ninth and tenth are the only compound terms generally used; and the terms for the simple intervals are often employed for all compound intervals.

Ex. 3.

Tenth or Third.   Twelfth or Fifth.

All intervals are reckoned *upwards*.

5. The intervals of the third (major or minor), perfect fifth, sixth (major or minor), and perfect octave are said to be consonant. Those of the second, fourth, and seventh are dissonant.

When two parts take the same sound (i. e. at the same pitch) they are said to employ the Unison.

Ex. 4.

6. The student must be able to state accurately any intervals played from I, as in Ex. 2. Next he must take the other degrees of the scale as starting-points, and name accurately the qualities of the intervals.

The difference between the qualities of intervals taken from II, as compared with those taken from I, can be easily appreciated by taking into consideration what the intervals from II would be if it were regarded as a new Tonic.

Ex. 5.

Intervals from C as I :

| Major Second. | Major Third. | Perfect Fourth. | Perfect Fifth. | Major Sixth. | Major Seventh. | Perfect Eighth. |

Intervals from D as I :

| Major Second. | Major Third. | Perfect Fourth. | Perfect Fifth. | Major Sixth. | Major Seventh. | Perfect Eighth. |

Intervals from D as II :

| Major Second. | Minor Third. | Perfect Fourth. | Perfect Fifth. | Major Sixth. | Minor Seventh. | Perfect Eighth. |

Thus from D to F is a minor third,

,,   D to C   ,,   seventh,

both being a semitone less than the third and seventh from D as a Tonic (scale of D major).

The others are given below with the differences noted.

Ex. 6.

Intervals from E as III :

| Minor Second. | Minor Third. | | | Minor Sixth. | Minor Seventh. | |

Intervals from F as IV :

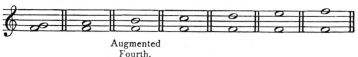

Augmented Fourth.

Intervals from G as V :

Minor
Seventh.

Intervals from A as VI :

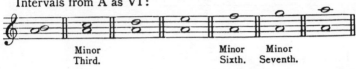

Minor
Third.

Minor
Sixth.

Minor
Seventh.

Intervals from B as VII :

Minor
Second.

Minor
Third.

Diminished
Fifth.

Minor
Sixth.

Minor
Seventh.

Thus a student should be able to sing or take down from dictation examples such as follow, I being in every case given beforehand : (*a*) II to VII, (*b*) III to VI, (*c*) IV to VII, (*d*) V to I¹.

7. When intervals beyond the octave are used the following abbreviations are useful :

$$I^1, II^1 = \text{octave above I or II},$$
$$I_1, II_1 = \text{octave below I or II},$$

and they can be referred to as higher I or lower II, &c.

Ex. 7.

Key C.

    v   II¹   v   VII₁   I

8. The following are examples of ear-tests.

No student should proceed to the next chapter till he is tolerably certain of the ground covered in this chapter.

EAR-TESTS.

Ex. 8.

Key G. Melodic.

Key D.

Key A.

Key F. Harmonic.

Key F.

Key F.

The master can devise similar tests in all the major **keys.**

CHAPTER II

PRIMARY TRIADS OF THE MAJOR KEY IN ROOT POSITION

1. IF we take I as a bass or lowest note and place above it (a) the third from I, (b) the fifth from I, the resultant combined sound is termed a triad.

Ex. 9.
Key C.

The lowest note (C) is termed the root. A triad formed by placing above a root the major third and perfect fifth from such root is called a Major Common Chord.

There are three such diatonic chords in the major key: Ia, IVa, and Va (a signifies root position of chord).

Ex. 10.

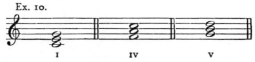

They are termed the Primary Triads of the key.

2. Having given the key-note, the master should play these in any order on the pianoforte, the student stating each chord as played. IVa can be distinguished from Va from the fact that Va contains the leading note (VII). They should all be distinguished from one another by listening to the pitch of the root.

The student must have no hesitation in distinguishing between I, IV, and V.

Ex. 11.
Key C major.

He should also sing the sounds forming the common chords on these notes.

$$I a \ (I + III + V).$$
$$IV a \ (IV + VI + I').$$
$$V a \ (V + VII + II').$$

3. The upper sounds forming the chords can be inverted in their positions.

Ex. 12.

4. These chords should now be arranged for voices (Soprano, Alto, Tenor, and Bass).

The compass of the various voices is approximately:

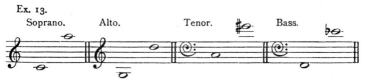
Ex. 13.
Soprano.   Alto.   Tenor.   Bass.

S. and A. are written in the treble stave, T. and B. in the bass stave.

Ex. 14.

5. As there are four voices and only three sounds in each chord, one factor of the chord must be sounded by two voices at the unison, octave, or fifteenth.

It is generally inadvisable to double the major third from the root; and the leading note should not be doubled. Therefore, double the root or fifth.

Adjacent parts should not be more than an octave apart, except the two lowest.

The following are good arrangements of I*a*:

Ex. 15.

6. Sometimes the fifth from the root may be omitted; the third should only be omitted for special effect.

Ex. 16.

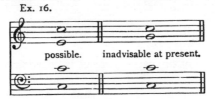

possible.   inadvisable at present.

7. Add parts for A. and T. to the following S. and B., forming primary triads. The parts must not cross, i.e. S. must be the highest part, A. the next, T. the next, and B. the lowest part.

Ex. 17.

8. Add parts for S. A. and T. to the following bass notes, forming primary triads. Give at least two arrangements of each.

Ex. 18.
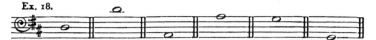

9. When a soprano part is given, to which parts for A. T. B. have to be added, there is scope for variety of choice.

At present the bass note can only be the root of the chord, but any higher part can be the root third or fifth of the chord.

Limiting ourselves to I*a*, IV*a*, and V*a*, a soprano C (in C major) could be the root of I*a*, or the fifth of IV*a*.

Ex. 19.

I*a*   IV*a*

A soprano G might be the root of V*a* or the fifth of I*a*.

Ex. 20.

V*a*   I*a*

But under the present limitations, a soprano E could only be the third of I*a*, and a soprano B only the third of V*a*, and a soprano F only the root of IV*a*, &c.

Ex. 21.

10. Add parts for A. T. B. to the following soprano notes forming Primary Triads (add the bass first, and then fill in the

middle parts). Harmonize each note in as many ways as are at present possible.

Ex. 22.

Key G.

11. Next we have to consider how to use these chords consecutively.

The following points must be memorized:

(*a*) A note common to two consecutive chords should generally be kept in the same part.

Ex. 23.

(*b*) A part should generally aim at moving to the next nearest note.

Ex. 24.

(*c*) Parts should not overlap; for example, the tenor in one chord should not be lower than the bass in the next chord (except between two positions of the same chord).

Ex. 25.

(*d*) No part should leap a seventh, or any compound inter-val (nor the latter with one note between).

Ex. 26.

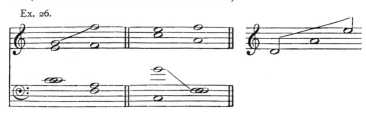

(*e*) No part must leap an augmented fourth; the leap of a diminished fifth may be used, if the next move be inside the interval.

Ex. 27.

bad   possible

(*f*) The leap of an octave should be preceded and followed by notes inside the interval.   The same often applies to the leap of the sixth.

Ex. 28.

bad   bad   tolerable

(*g*) The leading note should rise, except in changing to another position of the same chord (or in coming down the scale).

Ex. 29.

(*h*) No two parts should move in consecutive different chords in parallel perfect fifths or octaves.

Ex. 30.

(*i*) The extreme parts (S. and B.) should only approach an octave or fifth by similar motion if the S. move by step.

Ex. 31.

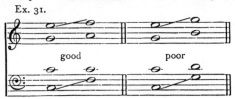

good   poor

When the top part leaps to the octave or fifth in similar motion with the bass, the octave or fifth is brought into undue prominence, and the octave or fifth is said to be exposed.

Recommendation. When *any* two parts approach an octave by similar motion, it is generally better for the higher of the two parts to move by step.

12. (1) V*a* to I*a* forms the Perfect Cadence, or Full Close, and is the general means of concluding a sentence; the final chord generally occurs on a strong accent.

Ex. 32.

(2) Chord IV*a* preceding these forms a good approach to the Cadence. When chords are used in root position a step apart, it is expedient to make the upper parts move if possible in contrary motion with the bass, so as to avoid such faults as consecutives and overlapping.

Ex. 33.

(3) I*a* to V*a*, or IV*a* to V*a* form a Half-close, or Imperfect Cadence ; this idiom is frequently used for the conclusion of any phrase except the last. The final chord generally occurs on a strong accent.

Ex. 34.

(4) IV*a* to I*a* forms the Plagal Cadence, which may be used at the end of any phrase, or as an extension of a Full Close.

Ex. 35.

(5) IV*a* forms a good approach to the Half-close.

(6) When V*a* is followed by IV*a*, let the soprano have the fifth of V*a* leaping up to the root of IV*a*.

13. All the examples in the preceding paragraph should be memorized, and taken down from dictation. At this stage it is all-important that the soprano and bass parts be heard accurately, and the chords recognized. It does not matter so much if the distribution of the middle parts is not accurately heard, though the student should be able to hear them tolerably well. For example, he should realize the difference in effect between the following:

The student should easily recognize the position of the third of the chord. If it is low down, the effect is somewhat thick and grumpy.

Exercises.

(1) Add parts for A. and T.:

Ex. 39.

(2) Add parts for S. A. T. (add S. first):

(3) Write for S. A. T. B.:

(a) Perfect Cadences in A major, F major, B flat major.

(b) Imperfect Cadences in D major, F sharp major, E flat major.

(c) Plagal Cadences in E major, A flat major, G major.

(d) Perfect followed by Plagal Cadences in D major, B flat major.

(e) IVa, Va, Ia in C major; IVa, Ia, Va in C major.

(4) Add parts for A. T. B. (add the bass first).

(a) Perfect Cadences:

(b) Imperfect Cadences:

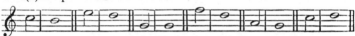

(c) Plagal Cadences:

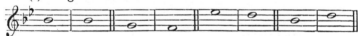

(d)

(e)

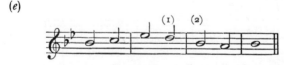

(1) Avoid using the same chord from a weak to a strong accent.

(2) Avoid Tonic chord in root position on the strong accent preceding the full close.

CHAPTER III

PRIMARY TRIADS OF THE MINOR KEY IN ROOT POSITION

1. For the present the harmony of the minor key will be derived exclusively from the harmonic minor scale.

Ex. 40.

C minor.

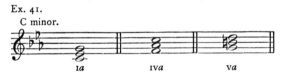

2. I*a* will consist of a bass note with the *minor* third and perfect fifth above it. This is called a Minor Common Chord, from the fact that the third above the root is minor.

Similarly, IV*a* is a Minor Common Chord.

But V*a* is the same chord as V*a* in the key of the Tonic major. The third will require an accidental sharpening it.

Ex. 41.

C minor.

Ia   iva   va

It will be observed that a harmonic minor scale differs from its Tonic major in the fact that III and VI are flattened.

3. The melodic interval of an augmented second is forbidden.

Ex. 42.

Thus the sixth and seventh degrees of the scale cannot occur as consecutive notes in the same part.

Ex. 43.

4. Sometimes the final I*a* of a piece in the minor key has the third sharpened so as to form a major common chord. This is called the Tierce de Picardie.

Ex. 44.

Writers of the sixteenth century never ended with a minor chord. They either sharpened the third, or left it out.

5. An accidental placed under a bass note means that the third from the bass note must be altered in accordance with the indication.

Ex. 45.

6. The following may be used as ear-tests, and as examples of the use of primary triads in the minor key.

Ex. 46.
Perfect Cadences.

Half-closes.

Plagal Cadences.

7. Exercises.

(1) Detect the faults in the following:

Ex. 47.

(2) Add parts for A. and T.:

(3) Add parts for S. A. T. (add S. first):

(4) Write for S. A. T. B. :

(a) Perfect Cadences in B minor, F minor, A minor (Tierce de Picardie).

(b) Imperfect Cadences in F sharp minor, E minor, D minor.

(c) Plagal Cadences in E minor, C minor, G minor (Tierce de Picardie).

(d) Perfect followed by Plagal Cadences in F minor, D minor, E minor (Tierce de Picardie).

(e) IVa, Va, Ia in D minor ; IVa, Ia, Va in D minor ; Ia, Va, IVa, Ia in E minor.

(5) Add parts for A. T. B. (add the bass first) :

(a) Perfect Cadences :

(b) Imperfect Cadences :

(c) Plagal Cadences :

(d)

Perfect Cadence.   Plagal Cadence.

(e)

CHAPTER IV

IIA AND VIA IN THE MAJOR KEY; VIA IN THE MINOR KEY

1. In the major key, II*a*, III*a*, and VI*a* are minor common chords, and are termed secondary triads.

Ex. 48.
Key C.

II*a*   III*a*   VI*a*

III*a* is an edged tool, and should be omitted for the present.

VII*a* is a diminished triad, consisting of a root and its minor third and diminished fifth. It is a discord, and is likewise left over for future treatment.

Ex. 49.

VII*a*

2. II*a* followed by V*a*, or VI*a* followed by V*a*, form further varieties of the Half-close.

Ex. 50.

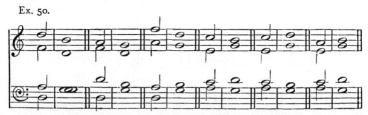

We now have the following forms of the Half-close:

        (*a*) I*a* to V*a*.
        (*b*) II*a* to V*a*.
        (*c*) IV*a* to V*a*.
        (*d*) VI*a* to V*a*.

If possible, avoid two parts moving by step of a tone in consecutive major thirds.

Ex. 51.

poor

They cause the 'false relation of the tritone' (F to B).

3. Va to VIa forms the False Cadence (also called the Deceptive or Interrupted Cadence). The progression avoids the expected Full Close.

Ex. 52.

4. It is at present inadvisable that the extreme parts in any case approach an octave or fifth by similar motion when one or both of the chords is a secondary triad.

Ex. 53.

It is generally better that the bass should leap a third downwards instead of a sixth upwards, or a third upwards instead of a sixth downwards.   Exceptions, of course, must occur.

As regards exposed fifths, the following progression is generally allowed between IIa and Va.

Ex. 54.

allowed

5. In using Ia, IIa, IVa, Va, VIa, the only progression that is really bad is from IIa to Ia. Chords having two notes in common (IIa and IVa; IVa and VIa) are better in effect when used from strong to weak, rather than from weak to strong, especially if the roots rise a third.

Ex. 55.

good   poor

6. Roots falling a third are in any case better in effect than roots rising a third, which are nearly always poor in relation of weak to strong but quite tolerable strong to weak.

Ex. 56.

good   good   good   good

But, of course, a great deal depends upon the context.

7. The following form good approaches to a Full Close:

               (a) IIa   Va   Ia.
               (b) IVa   Va   Ia.
               (c) VIa   Va   Ia.

Avoid Ia, Va, Ia, which anticipates the final bass note.

Ex. 57.

8. Good approaches to a False Close:

               (a) IIa   Va   VIa.
               (b) IVa   Va   VIa.
               (c) Ia   Va   VIa.

Ex. 58.

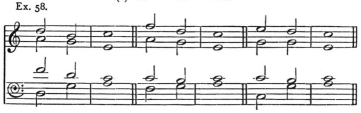

9. Good approaches to a Half-close:

(a) Ia	IVa	Va.	(f) IVa	VIa	Va.
(b) Ia	VIa	Va.	(g) VIa	IIa	Va.
(c) Ia	IIa	Va.	(h) VIa	IVa	Va.
(d) IVa	Ia	Va.	(i) IIa	IVa	Va.
(e) IVa	IIa	Va.	(j) IIa	VIa	Va.

Ex. 59.

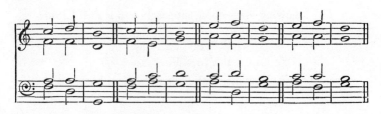

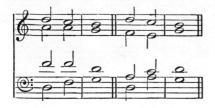

Experience has proved that such lists are necessary for average beginners. If left to their own initiative, they will probably choose any progressions except those given above. This might be a sign of intense originality, and of dislike of the commonplace; it usually has quite another meaning.

10. If the Plagal Cadence is not preceded by the Full Close, forming a sort of Coda—that is to say, if it is used as the end of a phrase, it is only satisfactorily preceded by VI*a*, or V*a*.

Ex. 60.

(That is, of course, under the limited conditions of this chapter.)

11. A consideration of cadences and their approach has practically exhausted the ordinary uses of the chords under consideration.

12. In the minor key VI*a* is the only other common chord

derivable from the harmonic minor scale. It is a major chord. In the major key VIa is minor.

Ex. 61.

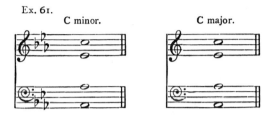

In proceeding from Va to VIa, or vice versa, the major third from the root in VIa must be doubled, in order to avoid faulty grammar.

Ex. 62.

Note: (a) The leading note rises one step.

(b) The major third in VIa is doubled.

(c) Contrary motion with the bass is used wherever possible.

13. We have now the following forms of the Half-close:

(a) Ia to Va.

(b) IVa to Va.

(c) VIa to Va.

Ex. 63.

14. The False Cadence is as follows:

Ex. 64.

15. The references to the use of IV*a* and VI*a* in the **major** key in paragraph 5 refer also to their use in the minor key.

16. VI*a* forms a new approach to the Full Close.

Ex. 65.

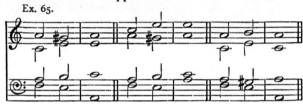

17. It will only be necessary to mention good approaches **to** a Half-close involving VI*a*:

    (*a*) I*a*   VI*a*   V*a*.
    (*b*) IV*a* VI*a*   V*a*.
    (*c*) VI*a* IV*a*   V*a*.

Ex. 66.

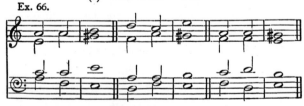

18. Approach of Plagal Close:

Ex. 67.

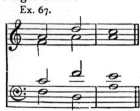

19. The examples of progressions should be used as ear-tests.

20. Exercises.

Ex. 68.

(1) Add parts for A. and T.:

In harmonizing melodies note:

(a) The same chord should not be used weak to strong except at the start

(b) Va to Ia should not be used weak to strong except at the beginning or the end.

(c) Ia should not immediately precede the Full Close.

(d) If a melody note be tied weak to strong, change the harmony on the strong accent.

(2) Add Basses, then A. and T.:

two different chords.

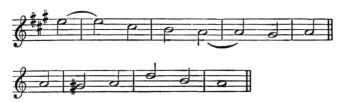

(3) Write (a) various forms of the Half-close for S. A. T. B. in the keys of D major and D minor.

(b) Full Closes preceded by another chord in the keys of F major, F minor.

(c) False Closes in G major, G minor.

(d) False Closes preceded by another chord in C major and C minor.

(e) Various forms of the Half-close preceded by another chord in A major, A minor.

(4) Fill in suitable chords in the blank spaces:

Half-Close   Full Close.

(5) Add parts for S. A. T.:

Phrase endings.

(6) Alter the final chords in *a*, *b*, *c*, *d* to form False Cadences.

CHAPTER V

FIRST INVERSIONS OF TRIADS IN THE MAJOR KEY

1. If the bass of each of the triads of the scale be transferred to a higher part, and the original third of the chord be left as the bass, we produce what are termed first inversions of the triads.

Ex. 69.

Key C major.

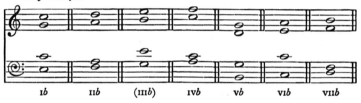

2. The principle of doubling is the same as in the case of chords in root position.

3. For the present we omit III*b*. VII*b* is included as its use is very common.

4. The ear must be at once trained to detect whether a bass note of a chord is a root or third, in other words, whether the chord is in the root position or first inversion. The following tests should prove sufficient :

Ex. 70.

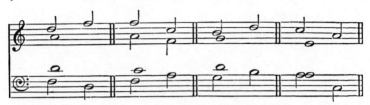

There should be no difficulty in determining whether the notes from the bass are at the diatonic intervals of 3 and 5, or 3 and 6. Separate first inversions should also be played, and the student should name them.

5. The following scheme shows the new resource available :

6 underneath a bass note signifies a first inversion and implies $\frac{6}{3}$. $\frac{5}{3}$ means the root position of a chord.

Ex. 71.

If the bass note be III, it must have as its figuring $\frac{6}{3}$. The same applies to VII. If the bass note be V, it must be $\frac{5}{3}$.

6. If a bass note proceed by diatonic steps from I to III, or from III to I, it is best to figure II as 6 (VII*b*).

Ex. 72.

And in this case the third from the bass in VII*b* should proceed in parallel thirds with the bass. And it is better not doubled. This is only a recommendation. (*a*) is better than (*c*). Teachers may explain that VII*b* is really the incomplete second inversion of the dominant seventh.

7. A $\frac{5}{3}$ followed by a $\frac{6}{3}$ on the same bass note is good strong to weak; some good following chords are given. It is always good to proceed to a $\frac{5}{3}$ or $\frac{6}{3}$ on the next note above; limiting the procedure by the facts that (a) the leading note must rise, (b) IIIa, IIIb, and VIIa are unavailable.

Much, of course, depends upon context. It is not desirable to attempt to exhaust possibilities.

Ex. 73.

Note in the above the treble is given the intervals 5 and 6 from the bass note.

8. Similarly, the following uses of $\frac{6}{3}$ to $\frac{5}{3}$ on the same bass note are good.

Ex. 74.

Other uses are not so good. Students should think out the reasons for themselves. They are connected with (a) the leading note, (b) the mental effect of the $\frac{5}{3}$ on a bass note preceded by a $\frac{6}{3}$.

9. Consecutive first inversions are good if the bass move by step. It is best for the soprano to move in sixths with the bass, and the inner parts should double alternately the root and fifth (except leading note).

Ex. 75.

10. A perfect fifth followed by a diminished fifth, or vice versa, may be used between two upper parts, if the lower of the two parts proceed by step of a semitone (e. g. between I*b* and VII*b*, not between VI*b* and VII*b*).

Ex. 76.

Thus when VI*b* and VII*b* are involved see that the parts concerned form consecutive fourths, and not fifths.

11. The use of a first inversion will give variety when a chord is repeated.

Ex. 77.

12. The judicious combination of root positions and first inversions will result in a more elegant bass part than when root positions only are used.

Ex. 78.

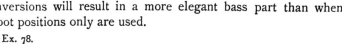

revised.

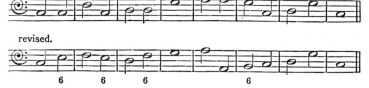

13. Roots falling a second are good in first inversions.

Ex. 79.

14. When the bass leaps a fourth or fifth both chords should generally be in root position, unless involving III*a* and VII*a*, which we omit in elementary work.

15. Do not use VII*b* to V*a*, the one kills the other.

Ex. 80.

V*a* to **VII***b* is good strong to weak.

Ex. 81.

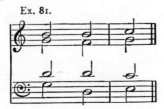

16. A triad in root position preceded by an available first inversion a step on either side is good, or vice versa.

Ex. 82.

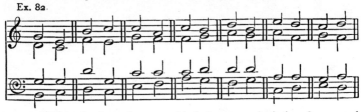

17. When the bass leaps a third downwards it is often good to use a first inversion for the second chord, though the choice must be limited by the succeeding chord. The choice of harmony must always be influenced by the particular context.

Ex. 83.

18. New approaches to the Perfect Cadence.

Ex. 84.

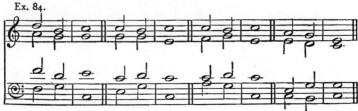

19. New approaches to the False Cadence.

Ex. 85.

20. New approaches to the Half-close, and new harmony for first chord of the Cadence.

Ex. 86.

21. New approaches to the Plagal Cadence.

Ex. 87.

All the above must be used as ear-tests.

22. Exercises.

Ex. 88.

(1) Add parts for S. A. T. to the following bass notes in various arrangements :

(2) Add parts for A. T. B., forming various available first inversions :

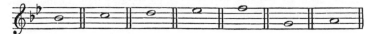

(3) Add parts for A. T. :

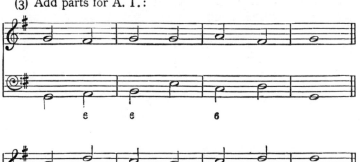

(4) Figure the following basses, and then add parts for S. A. T.:

(5) Add parts for A. T. B.:

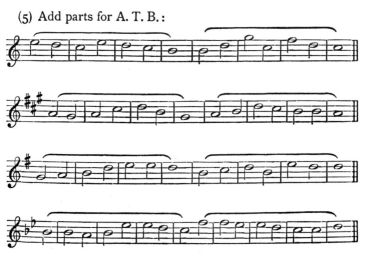

(6) Complete the following with suitable chords:

(7) Write in each example four chords, the last two producing cadences as follows:

(a) Half-close in F major, (b) Full Close in A major, (c) Plagal Close in C major, (d) False Close in D major.

Write as many varieties of each as occur to you.

CHAPTER VI

SOME FIRST INVERSIONS IN THE MINOR KEY

1. The following first inversions are at present available: I*b*, II*b*, IV*b*, V*b*, VI*b*, VII*b* (harmonic minor scale).

Ex. 89.

Key A minor.

2. If we compare these with the same chords in the tonic major key, we find the following differences:

Major Key.	Tonic Minor.
I*b*, major.	I*b*, minor.
II*b*, minor.	II*b*, diminished.
IV*b*, major.	IV*b*, minor.
VI*b*, minor.	VI*b*, major.

Note the following points:

Ex. 90.

The point to remember is, avoid the interval of the augmented second in melody.

Also, avoid the melodic interval of the augmented fourth.

3. The following table shows available harmony in the minor key :

Ex. 91.

4. Following the plan of the preceding chapter, note the following uses :

(a) I*a*, VII*b*, I*b*, and vice versa.

Ex. 92.

(b) $\frac{5}{3}$ followed by 6 on same bass note.

Ex. 93.

(*c*) The converse.

Ex. 94.

(*d*) Consecutive first inversions.

Ex. 95.

(*e*) Triads in root position preceded by first inversion a step on either side (or vice versa).

Ex. 96.

(*f*) Bass leaping down a third, the second chord being a first inversion.

Ex. 97.

(g) New approaches to the Perfect Cadence.

Ex. 98.

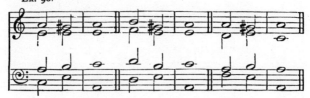

(h) New approaches to the False Cadence.

Ex. 99.

(i) New approaches to the Half-close, and new harmony for the first chord of the Cadence.

Ex. 100.

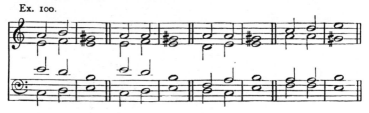

(j) New approaches to the Plagal Cadence.

Ex. 101.

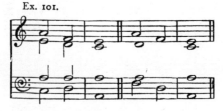

5. The majority of the other points mentioned in the previous chapter apply equally well here.

6. All the above examples should be used as ear-tests.

7. Exercises.

Ex. 102.

(1) Add parts for S. A. T. to the following bass notes in various arrangements:

(2) Add parts for A. T. B., forming various available first inversions:

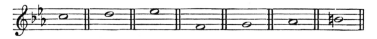

(3) Add parts for A. T.:

(4) Figure the following basses, and then add parts for S. A. T. :

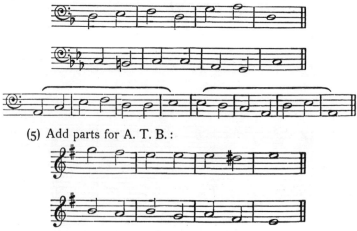

(5) Add parts for A. T. B. :

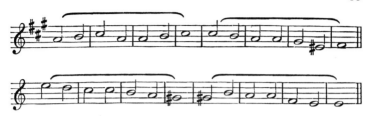

(6) Complete the following with suitable chords:

(7) Write in each example four chords, the last two producing Cadences as follows: (a) Half-close in F minor, (b) Full Close in A minor, (c) Plagal Close in C minor, (d) False Close in D minor.

Write as many varieties of each as occur to you.

CHAPTER VII

THE MELODIC MINOR SCALE

1. In order to avoid the melodic interval of the augmented second, the sixth degree of the scale may be sharpened in ascending, and the seventh degree of the scale flattened in descending the scale.

Ex. 103.

A minor.

2. For the present the use of chords involving the sharpened sixth and flattened seventh will be limited to cases in which one of the parts proceeds exactly as at *a*, *b*, *c*, or *d*.

3. The sharpened sixth can be harmonized as II with the perfect fifth, or IV with the sharpened third. The sharpened sixth should not be doubled. The minor sixth and major sixth must not occur in consecutive chords, nor should the major sixth occur in consecutive chords at present.

Ex. 104.

4. The flattened seventh can be harmonized as III or V or VII. The seventh can be doubled so long as one part proceeds as in *c* or *d*. The next chord but one should contain the major seventh. The major seventh and minor seventh must not occur in consecutive chords, nor should the minor seventh occur in consecutive chords at present.

Ex. 105.

5. In the following example the appearance of the major seventh is deferred, as another part is also using the melodic minor scale.

Ex. 106.

All the above should be used as ear-tests.

6. Exercises.

(1) Fill in appropriate chords in the blank spaces :

Ex. 107.

(a)

(2) Add A. and T. :

(3) Harmonize the following for S. A. T. B. :

(4) Figure the following basses, and add parts for S. A. T. :

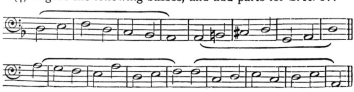

CHAPTER VIII

UNACCENTED DIATONIC PASSING NOTES: MAJOR KEYS

1. **When** consecutive harmony notes are a third apart, the intermediate step may be filled up by a diatonic note. Such a note is foreign to the harmony of the chords it connects, and is called generically an unessential note, in particular a passing note, as it passes on to a new harmony note.

Ex. 108.

2. At *a* we have the second of the scale of the first chord used as an ascending passing note.

At *d* we have it as a descending passing note.

At *b* we have the fourth of the scale of the first chord used as an ascending passing note.

At *e* the same as a descending passing note. The fourth of the scale of the chord, if descending to the third is harsh with the third heard against it. The bad effect is removed by the bass taking another passing note moving in parallel thirds with the soprano (*f*).

At *c* we have the seventh of the scale of the chord used as a descending passing note.

3. The sixth of the scale may also be used as a passing note, but it is better treated as a new concord, except in the progressions I*a*—V*a*; IV*a*—I*a*.

Ex. 109.

4. Two parts may use different passing notes together if they move in parallel thirds and sixths. A passing note cannot remain to be a new harmony note.

Ex. 110.

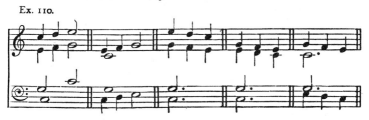

5. Two parts may take the same passing note by contrary and conjunct movement.

Ex. 111.

6. For the present, the use of two passing notes in succession is limited to progressions starting with I*a* or IV*a* (from the fifth

of the root in each case ascending or from the root to the fifth descending), and no other notes must be struck against either passing note.

Ex. 112.

7. If the introduction of a passing note produces fifths, it must be eliminated, or the passage re-arranged.

Ex. 113.

8. Passages incorrect without the use of passing notes are incorrect with them.

Ex. 114.

9. (*a*) Avoid the unison by oblique motion.

Ex. 115.

(*b*) Avoid quitting a second by similar motion.

Ex. 116.

The writing is congested.   Amend thus:

Ex. 117.

(*c*) Do not strike harmony notes with the second and fourth of the scale of the chord as passing notes.

Ex. 118.

The teacher may explain to the beginner the following if he deems it desirable:

Ex. 119.

10. In this chapter passing notes are unaccented, that is, they occur either as subsidiary parts of beats or as weak beats.

Ex. 120.

11. Exercises.

N.B.—Do not quit two unessential thirds or sixths in contrary motion.

(1) Re-write the following sections, introducing passing notes in the parts where appropriate :

Ex. 121.

2. Add parts for A. and T. Treat all unaccented crotchets approached and quitted by step as passing notes.

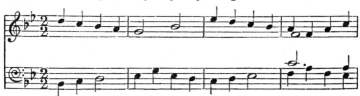

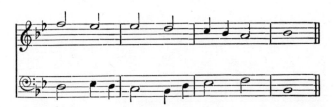

3. Harmonize the following for S. A. T. B. (add passing notes here and there in the added parts).   Unaccented quavers approached and quitted by step are passing notes.

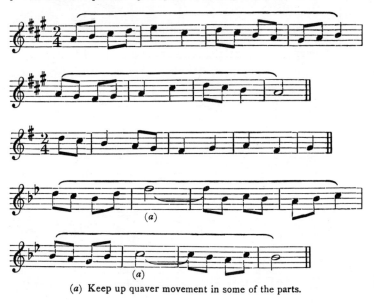

(a) Keep up quaver movement in some of the parts.

4. Add parts for S. A. T. :

A horizontal line means that the sounds indicated by the figures preceding it are to be retained so long as the line is continued. If the chord or use of unessential notes require no figures, the line starts with the note bearing the $\frac{5}{3}$.

5. Figure the bass of the following fully in accordance with the added parts:

6. Add S. to the following basses; figure them, treating appropriate crotchets as passing notes: maintain a fairly even flow of crotchet movement.

CHAPTER IX

UNACCENTED DIATONIC PASSING NOTES.
MINOR KEYS

1. THE necessity of avoiding the melodic interval of the augmented second between the sixth and seventh degrees of the harmonic minor scale causes some curious irregularities.

(*a*) The minor seventh of the scale of the tonic is used both as an *ascending* and descending passing note when using chords IV and VI.

Ex. 122.
A minor.

(*b*) The major sixth of the scale of the tonic is used not only as an ascending passing note over chords I and V, but also as a descending passing note between two positions of V.

Ex. 123.

2. Two passing notes in succession can be used over I and VI with the same limitations as in the major key.

Ex. 124.

3. Ear-tests.

Ex. 125.

A minor.

4. The ninth of a chord descending to the fifth of the next chord is ugly if foreign to the scale of the second chord (harmonic form).

Ex. 126.

5. Exercises.

(1) Re-write the following, adding appropriate passing notes:

Ex. 127.

D minor.

(2) Add parts for A. T., adding passing notes here and there:

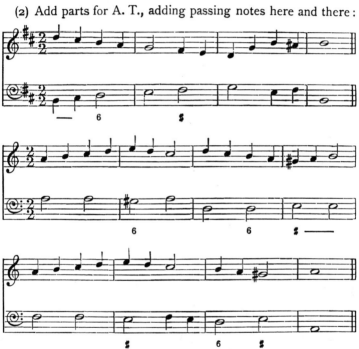

(3) Harmonize the following for S. A. T. B., adding appropriate passing notes:

(4) Figure the following basses, and add parts for S. A. T.:

(5) Add parts for A. T.:

CHAPTER X

THE CHORD OF THE SIX-FOUR

1. THE second inversion of the common chord is called the chord of the six-four, because it consists of a bass note, its fourth and sixth. It is figured $\frac{6}{4}$.

Ex. 128.

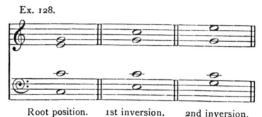

Root position.   1st inversion.   2nd inversion.

2. This chord is very restricted in its use, and it can only be employed upon certain degrees of the scale. It will be best to consider the chord under classified headings.

3. (a) *Cadential six-four.*

This is only used on the dominant and tonic notes.

It resolves into a $\frac{5}{3}$ on the same bass note,

    the sixth falls to the fifth,

    the fourth ,, third,

    the bass note is doubled in both chords.

Ex. 129.

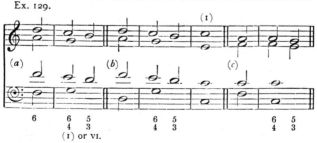

It will be felt that in all these cases the sixth and fourth are

appoggiaturas of the fifth and third. The six-fours are decorative, and are harmonic embellishments of:

Ex. 130.

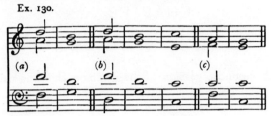

Thus they are decorative forms of the half, perfect, deceptive,
and plagal close.

In these cases the bass of the six-four cannot be approached
by leap from an inversion of another chord.

Ex. 131.

In the half and plagal closes the $\frac{6}{4}$ decorates the final chord,
in the perfect and false closes the $\frac{6}{4}$ decorates the penultimate
chord; and it must be more strongly accented than the succeeding $\frac{5}{3}$.   (Ic = second inversion of tonic chord.)

4. (*b*) *Passing six-four.*

This is only used as an intermediate chord between Ia and
Ib, or vice versa, and between IVa and IVb, or vice versa. The
soprano takes the same notes as the bass in the reverse order.

Ex. 132.

At (*a*) and (*b*) it is always preferable to use a ⁶₃ on D rather than a ⁶₄, if the choice is left to the student.

Ex. 133.

5. (*c*) *Auxiliary six-four.*

In this the bass remains stationary; and a ⁶₄ is used between two statements of the ⁵₃ on the same bass note.

This use is confined for the present to tonic and dominant basses.

Ex. 134.

6. (*d*) *Arpeggio six-four.*

In this case the bass moves to the six-four from the root position or first inversion of the same chord. If it proceed on to the root position or first inversion again, the bass is free to move as from that note. If, however, the bass move from the second inversion to another chord, it must proceed by step to another ⁵₃ or ⁶₃.

Ex. 135.

The six-four of I, II, IV, V, and VI can be thus used:

Ex. 136.

7. Observe the following points:

(a) Do not use the $\frac{6}{4}$ on the strong accent unless resolving into a $\frac{5}{3}$ on the same bass note.

Ex. 137.

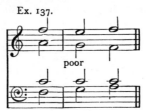

poor

(b) Do not use the $\frac{6}{4}$ as the first position of a chord.

Ex. 138.

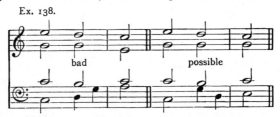

bad   possible

(c) Do not use the $\frac{6}{4}$ as the last chord upon a bass note, unless both the sixth and fourth move on to new harmony notes.

Ex. 139.

clumsy   good

$\frac{6}{3}$ $\frac{6}{4}$ 6

In this case regard the fourth and sixth as passing notes, and treat the bass as from the previous concord.

8. Consecutive six-fours may be used in two cases:

(a) When the bass is a broken form of the harmony of a passing six-four.

Ex. 140.

(b) When a passing six-four between Ib and Ia is followed by an appoggiatura $\frac{6}{4}$ to Ia.

Ex. 141.

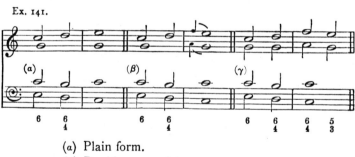

(a) Plain form.
(β) Double appoggiaturas.
(γ)   „   „   written as played.

9. The various examples of the different kinds of six-four should be used as ear-tests. The student should be sparing in the use of the six-four chord.

10. When the cadential six-four is used it may be preceded by another position of the same chord on the previous weak accent. The student should think out for himself the reason for this.

Ex. 142.

11. Exercises.

Ex 143

(1) Re-write the following, adding cadential six-fours:

(2) Re-write the following, adding passing six-fours:

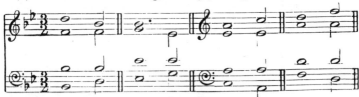

(3) Re-write the following, introducing auxiliary six-fours:

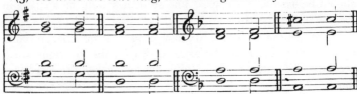

(4) Add arpeggio six-fours in the bass:

(5) Add another six-four to the following:

(6) Add parts for A. and T., taking care to use the **six-four** correctly:

(7) Harmonize the following for S. A. T. B. :

(8) Add parts for S. A. T. :

(9) Add A. and T. :

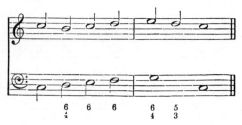

(10) Add S. A. T. to the following unfigured basses :

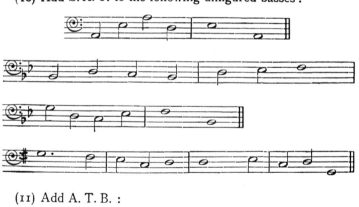

(11) Add A. T. B. :

CHAPTER XI

ACCENTED PASSING NOTES

1. Sometimes passing notes, instead of being struck alone between the chords, are struck with the chords and then resolve into them.

Ex. 144.

In the above example, *a*, *b*, *c*, and *d* are accented passing notes.

2. Do not strike the discord against the note into which it resolves except (*a*) the latter be in the bass, (*b*) by contrary and conjunct movement. The second exception should be rarely used. The fourth struck against the third of the chord is very harsh, and should be avoided.

Ex. 145

3. Accented passing notes are best in effect descending. They should be rarely used in the bass.

The only accented passing notes ascending used in this chapter will be in parallel thirds between the third and fifth, and root and third of the same chord, or with two parts using the same passing note in contrary motion (Ex. 147).

Ex. 146.

4. When the choice of harmony is left to the student, he must select as essential notes those that give the best progressions.

For example, at *c* in Ex. 144, if F had been chosen as the harmony note, V*a* to IV*a* is poor as compared with V*a* to I*b*.

If the given part leap from the second of two conjunct quavers, obviously the second is the harmony note.

Ex. 147.

No one with any musical sense would harmonize both quavers.

5. The student must get into the habit of mind of regarding many accented notes as being unessential.

Ex. 148.

6. The examples may be used as ear-tests.

Students should name or take down (*a*) the soprano part, (*b*) the bass, and then should name the chords, and if possible add the inside parts.

7. Exercises.

(1) Add accented passing notes in the soprano part of the following :

Ex. 149.

(2) Add ascending accented passing notes in soprano and bass (in parallels): see Ex. 146.

(3) Harmonize the following, using some accented quavers and crotchets as passing notes:

(4) Figure the following basses, and add soprano part.

The figures below a note show the actual intervals written above that note:

CHAPTER XII

THE CHORD OF THE DOMINANT SEVENTH

1. IF the minor seventh from the root be added to chord V, we produce the chord of the dominant seventh. It is figured 7 (V*a* 7). It is the same in both the major and minor key.

Ex. 150

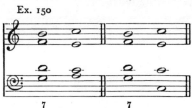

The seventh is a discord and must proceed one step downwards in the next chord. It therefore resolves into VI*a* or I*a* from the root position.

2. No two parts may proceed in similar motion from a seventh to an octave.

Ex. 151.

3. The seventh may be ornamentally resolved by proceeding first to some other factor of the chord. The fifth of the chord may be omitted.

Ex 152.

4. The resolution of the seventh may be transferred to some other part. In that case the part that originally had the seventh must fall.

Ex. 153.

5. Exceptionally, the seventh may remain to be a part of another chord.

Ex. 154.

6. As there are four notes in the chord, there are three inversions. They are given below with their resolutions. They all resolve on to the tonic chord.

Ex. 155.

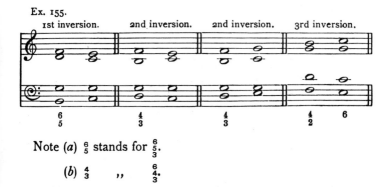

Note (a) $\frac{6}{5}$ stands for $\frac{6}{5}$.
      (b) $\frac{4}{3}$,, $\frac{6}{4}$.
      (c) $\frac{4}{2}$,, $\frac{6}{4}$.

(*d*) In the second inversion the seventh may rise a step in parallels with the bass.

(*e*) The bass of the second inversion is under the same restrictions as the bass of a six-four. But this $\frac{6}{4}$ can be used in a less restricted way than the plain $\frac{6}{4}$ of the dominant.

Ex. 156.

(2) and (3) are examples. The bass of a second inversion may be approached by leap from the root position of another chord.

(*f*) The same bass note may be used weak to strong, if the strong note be the seventh of a new chord.

Ex. 157.

(*g*) The approach of the bass of the third inversion is under no restrictions except those of good taste.

(*h*) Two parts should not approach the ninth (formed by the root and seventh) in similar motion.

Ex 158.

The seventh stands in place of the root. But the approach of the seventh in similar motion is not so objectionable.

Ex. 159.

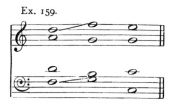

(*i*) The following idiom should be memorized:

Ex. 160.

(*j*) the $\frac{4}{2}$ forms a new way of following I*c*.

Ex. 161.

The fourths between the bass and tenor are good, the second fourth being augmented, and a substitution for a major third (G to B).

Ear-training.

Ex. 162.

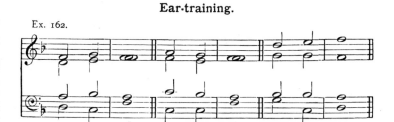

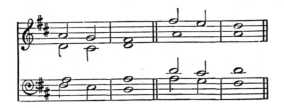

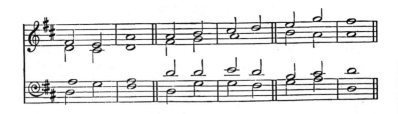

Exercises.

(1) Resolve the following chords:

Ex. 163.

(2) Precede and follow these chords by one chord on each side:

(3) In the blank spaces place chords of the dominant seventh:

Key C major.

(4) Add ornamental resolutions of the seventh:

N.B.—Avoid:

(5) Add parts for A. T.:

(6) Harmonize the following for S. A. T. B. :

* Let the bass leap a seventh from C to B flat ; a part may do this in arpeggio of the same chord.

(7) Figure the following basses, and add parts for S. A. T. ; introduce some passing notes :

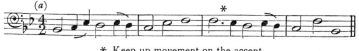

* Keep up movement on the accent.

CHAPTER XIII

DIMINISHED TRIADS IN ROOT POSITION: AUGMENTED TRIADS IN ROOT POSITION AND FIRST INVERSION

1. DIMINISHED Triads in root position occur on VII in the major key, and on II and VII in the minor key:

Ex. 164.

2. The diminished fifth from the bass is a discord and must occur in the same part in the previous chord. This is termed its preparation. It must resolve one step downwards into a concordance. VII*a* resolves into I*a*, and II*a* into V*a*.

Ex 165.

The diminished fifth must not be doubled.

3. When VII*a* in the major key occurs in the course of the repetition of a pattern called a sequence. it is free in its treatment.

Ex. 166.

4. The augmented triad occurs on III in the minor key. The augmented fifth from the bass should be prepared, and resolve one step upwards (being the leading note) into chord I, or VI.

Ex. 167.

5. The first inversion should be treated as a dominant chord with the sixth displacing the fifth. The seventh may be added, but it must be sounded below the sixth. Here we have new harmony for the Perfect and False Cadences.

Ex. 168.

At (b) the exposed octaves are harmless, for obvious reasons.

6. If the E flat in this chord be enharmonically changed to D sharp, we have an augmented triad on the dominant in the major key.

Ex. 169.

Here again D sharp is a substitution for D natural, but its tendency is to rise, not to fall.

It is an example of a chromatically altered chord. Its use for the present will be limited to the following idioms:

Ex. 170.

The seventh may be added to the chord, but it must be sounded *below* the altered fifth.

Ex. 171.

7. These chords should be very sparingly used, and it is sufficient for the present if the student understand their treatment.

Exercises.

Ex. 172.

(1) Write a chord on each side of the following:

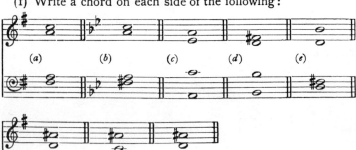

(2) Add parts for A. T.:

CHAPTER XIV

THE MEDIANT CHORD IN THE MAJOR KEY

1. In root position this chord should be preceded and followed by chords with which it has at least one note in common, except when used as a harmonization of the descending scale; in this case it may be followed by IV*a*.

Ex. 173.

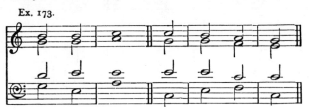

2. In the first inversion it may be preceded and followed (*a*) by a first inversion on either side, (*b*) or by chords with which it has at least one note in common.

Ex. 174.

3. But the first inversion may also be regarded as the dominant chord in root position with the fifth displaced. And in this light it may be used wherever the dominant could be employed, with the proviso that the sixth resolve a step or a third downwards.

Ex. 175.

4. The seventh may be added, but it must be sounded below the sixth.

Ex. 176.

5. The chord with or without the seventh forms new harmony for the Perfect and False Cadences.

Ex. 177.

6. The above examples should be used as ear-tests.

7. Exercises.

Ex. 178.

(1) Add parts for A. T. B., introducing III*a* and III*b* as in paragraphs 1 and 2:

(2) Add parts for A. T. B., introducing III*b* as a variation of dominant harmony:

(3) Introduce various uses of the mediant in the blank spaces, and fill in the harmony:

CHAPTER XV

AUXILIARY NOTES

1. An unessential note taken by step between two statements of the *same* harmony note is termed an auxiliary note.

Ex. 179.

2. Upper auxiliary notes, i. e. those lying above the harmony notes they connect, are diatonic. Avoid those above the fifth of II and root of III.

Ex. 180.

3. In the minor key use the harmonic minor scale in writing upper auxiliary notes over V and I.

Ex. 181.

va   1a

The minor seventh of the scale is used as an upper auxiliary note.

Ex. 182.
A minor.

VI a   IV a

4. Lower auxiliary notes:

(*a*) That below the root should be at the distance of a semitone from such note, unless in the next chord the harmony note leaps down a third, in which case the auxiliary note may be diatonic.

Ex. 183.

II a   V a   II a   V a

(*b*) Lower auxiliary notes of roots of diminished triads may be a tone or semitone below the root.

Ex. 184.

(*c*) The auxiliary note below the major third of a chord may be a tone or semitone from such note.

Ex. 185.

(*d*) The auxiliary note below the fifth of the root must be at the distance of a semitone, except when combined with that of the third. When the third is major, the fifth follows its procedure.

Ex. 186.

Except over IV, when *both* should be a semitone below.

Ex. 187.

IV

When the third is minor, the lower auxiliary note of the fifth may be either at the distance of a tone or semitone.

Ex. 188.

(*e*) When the lower auxiliary note of the root is combined with that of the third, if the former is diatonic the latter may be a tone or semitone below.

Ex 189.

When the former is chromatic, the auxiliary note of the third must be a semitone below.

Ex 190.

5. Auxiliary notes may be accented.

Ex. 191.

6. An auxiliary note, that is an unessential note a step above or below a harmony note, may be approached by leap.

Ex. 192.

When such a note is accented, it is called an appoggiatura.

Ex. 193

7. The examples may be used as ear-tests.

8. Exercises.

(1) Harmonize the following, regarding appropriate notes as being auxiliary :

Ex. 194.

(2) Re-write the following chords, adding any auxiliary notes you deem musical :

Key C major.

(3) Re-write the following, introducing auxiliary notes in the soprano and other parts (except bass):

(4) Write all the chords in D minor that you know, and decorate them in appropriate ways with auxiliary notes.

APPENDIX

PART I, CHAPTER XI

ADD:

Suppose a melody in the minor key contained the following progression :

Key A minor.

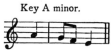

and it be intended to avoid modulation, the G♮ must be treated as an accented passing note :

For

(*a*) it is inartistic to harmonize both G and F, as they are notes of short duration ;

(*b*) G♮ is only used as a harmony note to reach F♮, a harmony note. If, therefore, G were the harmony note, and F the passing note, there would be no reason for substituting G♮ for **G♯.**

If the progression occurred after the first phrase, **and if** modulation were available, the following would be **correct**:

Modulation to C major.

It is not to be inferred from this that the following is incorrect:

But it must be understood that it is modal harmony (see *Evolution of Harmony*, Chap. II), and not a proper harmonization of the minor scale.

ELEMENTARY
HARMONY
PART II

BY

C. H. KITSON
M.A. Cantab., D.Mus. Oxon.

SOMETIME PROFESSOR OF MUSIC, UNIVERSITY COLLEGE, DUBLIN
SENIOR PROFESSOR OF THEORY, ROYAL IRISH
ACADEMY OF MUSIC, DUBLIN

OXFORD   NEW YORK
OXFORD UNIVERSITY PRESS

PREFACE

THIS part concludes diatonic harmony. It has been necessary to discuss some chromatic harmony, but only a very limited amount—e.g. that involved by the use of dominant fundamental harmony of the minor key in the major key, and by the employment of transition as opposed to gradual modulation. Part III will deal with chromatic harmony in general.

It is hoped that the use of various types of exercises will give the student the power to use the resource discussed in some practical fashion, and also give the mind the training that the figured bass denies. The Exercises have been made simple and short, as the students for whom this book is intended have not much time to devote to the subject. But it has been my aim to enable them to spend what little time they have to the best advantage.

C. H. KITSON.

CONTENTS

CHAPTER I

CHAPTER I

DIATONIC CHORDS OF THE SEVENTH

˳1. IF a diatonic seventh from the root be added to the diatonic triads of the key (except V), the resultant chords are
termed diatonic sevenths.

Ex. 1.
C major.

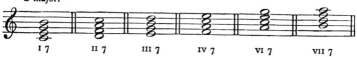

2. In employing these chords :

(*a*) The discord of the seventh must be 'prepared' by
occurring in the same part in the previous chord ;

(*b*) The discord must resolve one step downwards into a
chord of which such resolution is the third.

It will be obvious that IV 7 and VII 7 will be rarely used, as
IV will resolve into VII and VII into III. They are common
in the course of a sequence, e.g. a passage framed on at least
two chords, repeated at a different pitch (see ×).

Ex. 2.

3. If the third in one chord remains to be the seventh in the next, a chain of sevenths may be produced.

Ex. 3.

(*a*) The doubling of the leading note, as the result of the repetition of a pattern forming a sequence, is allowable.

4. First inversions need no extra explanation.

Ex. 4.

5. Second inversions are rare, because of the difficulty of satisfactory approach. Generally some other harmony is preferable.

Ex. 5.

The beginner is recommended to leave them alone. The bass of any second inversion is under the same restrictions as the bass of an ordinary six-four as regards the manner of approaching and quitting it.

6. Third inversions:

Ex. 6.

&c.

$$\frac{4}{2} \quad 6 \quad \frac{4}{2} \quad 6 \quad \frac{4}{2} \quad 6$$

7. Inversions resolving into other chords of the seventh:

Ex. 7.

$$\frac{6}{5} \quad \frac{4}{2} \quad \frac{6}{5} \quad \frac{4}{2} \qquad \frac{4}{2} \quad \frac{6}{5} \quad \frac{4}{2} \quad \frac{6}{5} \quad \frac{4}{2} \quad \frac{6}{5}$$

8. II 7 gives a new approach to the Perfect, False, or Imperfect Cadence.

Ex. 8.

9. **The Minor Key.**

Secondary sevenths involving the leading note are practically useless. Those involving the flattened leading note should not be attempted in elementary work. II 7 and VI 7 are the only diatonic sevenths that will be considered in this chapter.

Ex. 9.

10. As the cadential six-four is a decoration of the five-three into which it resolves, II 7 can proceed to this before finally resolving, the seventh remaining to be the fourth from the bass note in the six-four.   II 7 of the minor key is also available in the major key.

Ex. 10.

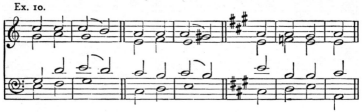

Ear·tests.

Ex. 11.

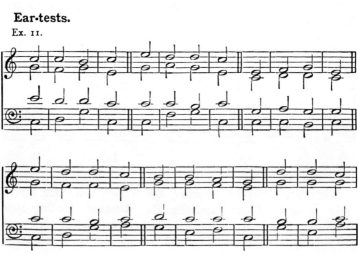

(*a*) Ornamental resolution.

Exercises.

(1) Add parts for A. and T., introducing some unessential notes:

(2) Add parts for A. T.:

(e)

(3) Harmonize the following Cadences, using the diatonic chord of the seventh on the supertonic in approaching them:

Perfect Cadence.   False Cadence.   Perfect Cadence.

Half-close.   Full Close.

(4) Continue the following sequences for a few bars, and end in an appropriate manner:

(5) Figure the following basses and add parts for S. A. T., introducing secondary sevenths and unessential notes:

(6) Precede and follow the given chords by other **chords in** the keys stated :

G major.

E minor.

(7) Harmonize the following for S. A. T. B., introducing diatonic chords of the seventh :

(a) Ornamental resolution.

(8) Continue the following sequences for a few bars, and conclude:

CHAPTER II

PARTICULAR USES OF SOME
DIATONIC SEVENTHS

1. II 7 in the first inversion can be used as if the sixth from the bass were added to IV*a*; for this reason it is called the chord of the added sixth. It can resolve on to I*a*.

Ex. 12.

The same procedure may be used with VI 7 in the first inversion.

Ex. 13.

In the minor key the sixth degree of the scale will be sharpened.

2. Provided that a discord resolve one step downwards, there is no fixed rule as to what chord shall form the resolution. Therefore:

(*a*) IV 7 may resolve into V, or V decorated by the six-four on its bass note.

Ex. 14.

Also in minor key.

In the first inversion the seventh should be sounded *above* the root, else the effect is unpleasant.   Other inversions are not recommended.

(*b*) VI 7 may resolve into a dominant seventh.

Ex. 15.

In the minor key the sixth degree of the scale is sharpened.

Ex. 16.

(c) VII 7 may resolve into a dominant seventh, or into the tonic chord.

Ex. 17.

In the major key, when resolving into the tonic chord, this is called the Chord of the Leading Seventh. In the minor key it is termed the Chord of the Diminished Seventh.

In the inversions, in the major key the seventh should be sounded above the root.

Ex. 18.

No two parts may proceed from 7 to 8.

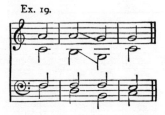

Ex. 19.

Observe that in all these cases a correct bass will move by
step or remain stationary in quitting the chord of the seventh.

3. In all these particular uses, the seventh of the root *may* be
taken without preparation.

Ex. 20.

4. The diminished seventh of the minor key may be used in
the tonic major key.

Ex. 21.

It is in this case a chromatic discord : that is to say, it contains a sound not found in the diatonic scale of the key. Designate the chord thus : VII$_{b7}$, or VII$_{\natural7}$, as the case may be.

Ear-tests.

All the examples of this chapter, except those illustrating faults, may be employed as ear-tests.

Exercises.

Ex. 22.

(1) Harmonize the following cadences, using the chord of the added sixth :

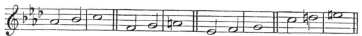

(2) Write chords to precede and follow the given chords in as many ways as you deem appropriate :

(3) Add parts for A. and T. :

(4) Harmonize the following in four parts, illustrating the particular uses of diatonic sevenths discussed:

(5) Figure and harmonize the following basses:

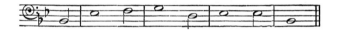

CHAPTER III

CHANGING NOTES, ANTICIPATIONS, AND CHROMATIC PASSING NOTES

1. Two statements of the same harmony note may be separated by the use of the unessential notes a step above and below
such harmony in either order.

Ex. 23.

But, when such harmony note is the root of the chord, the
lower unessential note must be a semitone below it, unless the
next harmony note be a third below the original one.

Ex. 23 a.

When such harmony note is the fifth of the chord, the lower
unessential note must be a semitone below it, unless the second
displaces the third as the fourth displaces the fifth.

Ex. 23 *b*.

ugly   good   good

2. Two harmony notes a third apart (the second being lower than the first) may be separated by the unessential note a step below the first, followed by that a step below the second.

Ex. 24.

(*a*)   (*b*)   (*c*)   (*d*)

The unessential note below the root must be a semitone from it, unless it falls a third to the succeeding harmony note (see (*c*) and (*d*)). In the following example the idiom is retained, but the third quaver is the harmony note. The fourth quaver should rise one step, according to ancient convention.

Ex. 25.

3. Two harmony notes a third apart (the second being higher than the first) may be separated by the unessential note a step above the first, followed by that a step above the second.

Ex. 26.

All these are examples of changing notes.

4. The two harmony notes connected by the changing notes may be factors of different chords.

Ex. 26 *a*.

5. When two harmony notes are a step apart, the second being lower than the first, the unessential note next above the first may leap down a third to the second.

Ex. 27.

Ex. 28.

6. Somewhat rarely the reverse procedure is employed.

Ex. 29.

7. These idioms must not be confused with the use of appog-giaturas.

Ex. 30.

8. The idiom explained in paragraph 1 may be curtailed by the omission of the initial note.

Ex. 31.

9. When two harmony notes are a step apart, the second may be anticipated over the harmony of the first. The note em-ploying this device is termed an anticipation. It is generally used in the top part, or in the top part combined with another. Do not strike other harmony notes with the anticipation.

Ex. 32.

10. Passing and auxiliary notes used between statements of the same chord may be anticipated.

Ex. 33.

11. Chromatic passing notes may be employed. Care must be taken that the chromatic semitone below the major third of the chord (used either as a passing note, appoggiatura, or auxiliary note) has not the effect of being the minor third.

Ex. 34.

It is generally agreed that, in order to ensure uniformity of style, once a chromatic passing note is introduced, the part must proceed in semitones till a harmony note is reached.

12. It is not good to alter a passing note chromatically to become a harmony note.

In the above example F cannot be regarded as being E sharp. We cannot chromatically raise the major third of a chord.

13. The collision of the major and minor thirds over dominant harmony in the minor key is allowed, thus:

Take care in such a case that the minor third is of quite short duration.

14. Ear-tests may be selected from the examples in this chapter.

Exercises.

(1) Re-write the soprano parts in the following, introducing the unessential resource indicated :

Ex. 39.

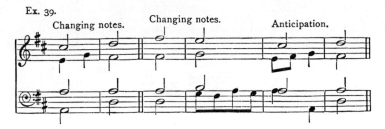

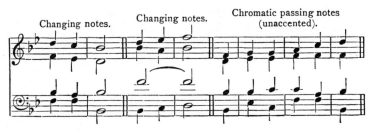

(2) Harmonize the following fragments in four parts :

(3) Add inner parts to the following:

(4) Add S. A. T. in accordance with the figures :

(5) Harmonize the following for S. A. T. B. :

CHAPTER IV

ELEMENTARY MODULATION. (*a*)

1. MODULATION is 'the process of passing out of one key into another' (GROVE).

A new key is established when the dominant of this key is followed by its tonic, provided that either contains a note foreign to the key quitted.

The following is not a modulation from C major to F major, because all the chords are diatonic in C major:

Ex. 40.

2. The process of modulation is carried out by approaching a chord as belonging to the first key and quitting it as belonging to the new key, and then adding the Perfect Cadence. A modulation from C major to F major would be produced (*a*) by adding the minor seventh to the dominant of F, or (*b*) by preceding this dominant chord by a chord belonging to F major but not to C major.

Ex. 41.
(*a*)   (*b*)

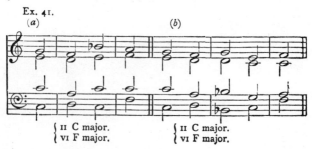

{ II C major.   { II C major.
{ VI F major.   { VI F major.

3. Although a key is only actually confirmed by dominant to tonic, yet it must be conceded that this direct confirmation is not always necessary or desirable. A False Close does not take away the effect of a new key, it merely avoids finality in it. The same may be said of the Half-close.

Ex. 42.

These procedures will give variety in cadences.

4. Generally speaking, the process of modulation is satisfactory if completed in at least four chords:

(*a*) The tonic chord of the first key.

(*b*) The pivot chord with the dual relation, being neither the tonic of the first key nor the tonic or the dominant of the second key.

(*c*) The dominant of the new key.

(*d*) The tonic of the new key.

Ex. 43.

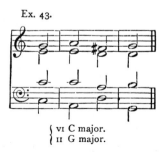

{ vi C major.
{ ii G major.

5. This chapter will be concerned with modulation to nearly related keys, e.g. tonic, dominant, and subdominant with their relatives:

		A minor.	E minor.	D minor.
C major.	Related keys.			
			G major.	F major.

		C major.	E minor.	D minor
A minor.	Related keys.			
			G major.	F major.

6. It is not always possible with the present resource to avoid the tonic of either key as the pivot chord :

(*a*) Modulation from C major to D minor.

D minor is the only diatonic chord with a dual relation.

(*b*) A minor to E minor.

A minor must be the pivot chord.

(*c*) A minor to G major.

A minor must be the pivot chord.

(*d*) A minor to D minor.

D minor must be the pivot chord.

Thus the process of modulation can be carried out in three chords, or in more than four.

Ex. 44.

C major to G major.

{ vi. C major.
{ ii. G major.

{ i C major.
{ iv G major.

{ vi C major.
{ ii G major.

C major to A minor.   C major to E minor.   C major to F major.

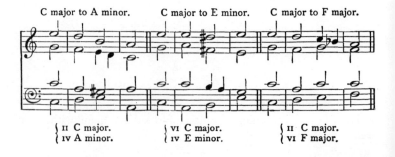

{ ii C major.
{ iv A minor.

{ vi C major.
{ iv E minor.

{ ii C major.
{ vi F major.

7. In modulating from a minor key to its subdominant minor (A minor to D minor) it is better to introduce at least one chord belonging to the new key after the pivot chord, to avoid the unpleasant juxtaposition of the major and minor forms of the same chord (A minor and A major).

Be careful to avoid such an ugly part as:

Ex. 45.

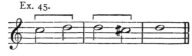

Put C natural and C sharp in different parts.

8. A modulation is usually confirmed at a cadence.

In harmonizing a melody, note that the melody may either express the modulation by having the necessary accidental, or imply it by its formation.

Ex. 46.

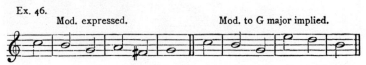

9. Sometimes the actual modulation is made in the course of a phrase and then confirmed with a Full Close at the end. In such a case avoid the new tonic in *root* position in the middle of the phrase on the strong accent.

In (*a*), I occurs in the root position on the weak accent.

In (*b*), I occurs in the first inversion on the strong accent.

In (*b*), V could have been followed by VI instead of I*b*.

10. If two modulations occur in a phrase, one during its course, and the other at the end, the former should have its I in the first inversion, or use V to VI.

Ex. 48.

11. When there is no chord common to the two keys, the modulation is termed abrupt; the procedure is also called a transition. In this case the connecting link is a note in common. This procedure is useful in the middle of phrases, except the first, or in sub-phrases. It should not be used at the end of normal phrases.

Ex. 49.

C major to A minor. C major to D minor.

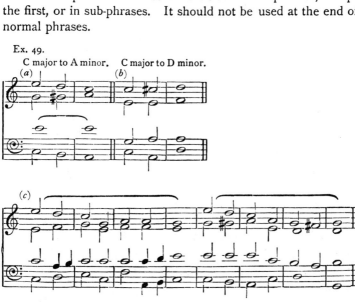

(*a*) and (*b*) are examples of transitions.

(*c*) gives two phrases, in the second there is a transition followed by a modulation.

(*d*) is an example of the bad use of transition.

12. Transitions provide opportunities for the use of sequence, the progression V to I being used in two or more keys.

When the qualities of the intervals forming the chords in each statement are the same, the sequence is real. This can occur when the two keys are both major or minor.

Ex. 50.

C major.   B♭ major.

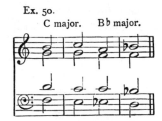

But when one key is major and another minor, or vice versa, the qualities of the intervals forming the chords cannot be exactly reproduced. The sequence is then free.

Diatonic sequences must be free.

Modulating sequences are either strict (real) or free.

Ex. 51.

C minor.   B♭ major.

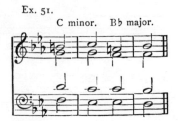

13. A section of melody such as follows often causes students trouble :

Ex. 52.
End of phrase.

(a)   (b)

(*a*) is obviously a modulation to G major. At (*b*), the only satisfactory treatment of B flat is to regard it as the seventh of the root C. Thus, if the major third of a chord be immediately chromatically flattened, treat the flattened note as a discord.

Ex. 53.

&c.

14. When the major or minor third of a chord is chromatically altered to become the minor or major third of the same chord, or the root or fifth of another chord (following it in consecutive order), such altered note must be kept in the same part, otherwise the unpleasant effect termed False Relation is produced.

Ex. 54.

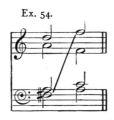

Bearing in mind the facts that (*a*) false relation is caused by placing in unpleasant juxtaposition chords that produce confusion of tonality, (*b*) the addition of the minor seventh to a major common chord does not alter its derivation, it will be obvious that the question of false relation does not enter into such a case as the following :

Ex. 55.

There is no false relation between the chords of G and C.

15. False relation is said to occur with a chord intervening as in the following case :

Ex. 56.

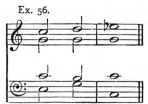

But the false relation is considered unobjectionable—

(*a*) in the Tierce de Picardie ;

(*b*) in using the minor seventh of the minor scale as a harmony note.

Ex. 57.

16. Ex. 44 should be used for ear-tests.

17. The exercises in this chapter will be concerned only with the processes of modulation and transition. Their application in framing sentences will be considered in the next chapter.

Exercises.

(1) Imitating the procedures in Ex. 44, modulate in a few chords from :—(a) F major to C major, (b) G major to E minor, (c) D major to F sharp minor, (d) D major to G major, (e) G major to A minor, (f) E minor to G major, (g) E minor to B minor, (h) B minor to A major, (i) B minor to E minor, (j) E minor to C major.

(2) Write transitions from (a) D major to E minor, (b) F major to D minor.

(3) Harmonize the following, introducing the modulations expressed or implied (the sections end with Full Closes in the new key; all begin in B flat major):

(1) Two ways, modulate to F major and to D minor.

(4) Harmonize the following, introducing the modulations expressed or implied (the sections end with Full Closes in the new key; all begin in F minor):

(5) Add parts for S. A. T. Modulations are anticipated in the course of the phrases, and confirmed at the end:

(6) Harmonize the following, introducing both transition and modulation in the same section:

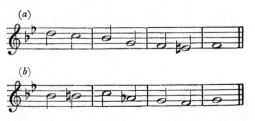

(7) Harmonize the following sections as modulating sequences:

(a)

G minor.   F major.

(b)

B♭ major.   G minor.

(8) Harmonize the following sections of bass:

(a) Diatonic sequence:

(b) Modulating sequence (free):

(c) Modulating sequence (strict):

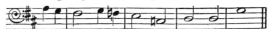

(d) Modulating sequence (free):

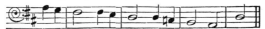

CHAPTER V

ELEMENTARY MODULATION. (*b*)

1. This chapter deals with the application of modulation in forming sentences or periods, or in harmonizing melodies or basses producing them.

A sentence in music consists of two phrases, each normally four bars long. This, however, is too short for any extended scheme of modulation.

If another sentence be added, sixteen bars in all, a cycle of modulations will be satisfactory in effect.

2. This period of sixteen bars is generally considered as divisible into two equal parts (Binary form). In deciding upon a scheme of modulation for the whole, the following points must be carefully borne in mind :

(*a*) The tonic key should be thoroughly established before modulation takes place. Therefore it is advisable not to modulate in the first phrase at all : a Full Close in the tonic at the end of the first phrase is quite possible.

(*b*) The second phrase should end with a Full Close in some key *not* on the flat side of the tonic. This modulation must be gradual, and it may be preceded by some other transition or modulation with its tonic in the first inversion, or any other appropriate means of avoiding finality.

(*c*) More frequent modulation may occur in the second half. Often the third phrase splits up into two smaller sections utilizing sequence. This is the place for modulation on to the flat side. Avoid new tonics in root position on the strong accents.

(*d*) The fourth phrase may have modulation at its outset, but time must be given to re-establish the tonic by gradual modulation.

Thus the following is a good scheme:

Bars 1-4, C major.

    ,,   5-8, through A minor to G major.

    ,,   9-12, F major, D minor.

    ,,   13-16, back to C.

Ex. 58.

3. In the above example all the modulations are confirmed by the use of V to I. This could be avoided sometimes, but not

always. At (*a*) a Half-close could have been used, but the dominant would have to be followed by the tonic, for the use of V to
VI would demand the chord of F major, which would make the
modulation to G major abrupt.

Ex. 59.

There could have been either a False Close or Half-close at
(*b*).   A False Close at (*c*) would be poor, as the chord of B flat
puts the mind off C major, which has to be re-established.

4. A diatonic passing note in the new key which is foreign to
the key quitted, cannot be introduced until the new key has been
established, in which case it will usually have been heard as an
essential note.

Ex. 60.
(*a*)

(*b*)

5. The following points must be carefully borne in mind in harmonizing melodies or unfigured basses:

(*a*) If a given part commences with chromaticisms, every effort must be made to avoid modulation:

Ex. 61.

(*b*) On the other hand, the end of the second phrase may have no chromaticism and yet demand modulation.

Ex. 62.

(*c*) If a melody begin with a phrase or section repeated, harmonize it first without modulation, and then with it.

Ex. 63.

(*d*) If a melody seems to allure one into a Full Close in the tonic in the middle of the problem, modulation or transition is generally possible.

Ex. 64.

Key C major.

End of phrase.   &c.   &c.

6. Exercises.

(1) Harmonize the following with appropriate modulations (S. A. T. B.):

None of the chromaticisms need imply modulation.

(a)

Chromatic notes imply modulation.

(b)

(2) Add parts for S. A. T., introducing suitable modulations:

(3) Following the plan of formation in the preceding exercises,

(*a*) Start as follows:

and proceed thus : bars 5–8, through B minor to F sharp minor ; 9–10, E minor ; 11–12, G major ; 13–16, back to D major.

(*b*) Start as follows :

and proceed thus : bars 5–8, through C major to E minor ; 9–10, F major ; 11–12, B flat major ; 13–16, back to A minor.

CHAPTER VI

SUSPENSIONS

1. WHEN a part that normally proceeds by one step downwards from an essential note in one chord to an essential note in another, retards its movement until the other factors of the second chord have been struck, the retarded note at this point is called a Suspension. Its occurrence in the same part in the previous chord is termed its preparation, and its final descent into the harmony of the second chord is termed its resolution.

Ex. 65.

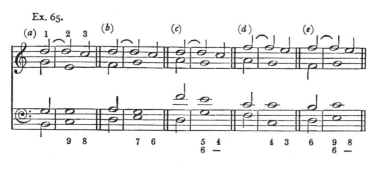

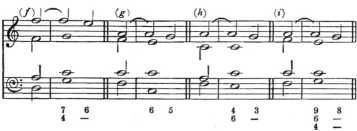

2. In the example (a) and in the further examples at the same

places, (1) is the preparation of the suspended discord, (2) is the suspension itself, (3) is its resolution.

3. In the examples (a), (b), and (c) the root of the chord is suspended, and the root position and two inversions are given. 9 8 implies $\frac{9\ 8}{5\ -}$; 7 6 implies $\frac{7\ 6}{3\ -}$.

4. In the examples (d), (e), (f) the third of the chord is suspended. 4 3 implies $\frac{4\ 3}{5\ -}$.

5. In (g), (h), and (i) the fifth of the chord is suspended. 6 5 implies $\frac{6\ 5}{3\ -}$.

6. The discord should not be sounded against its resolution, except the resolution be in the bass only, as at (a), (e), and (i).

Exceptionally the discord may be sounded against its resolution in an upper part by contrary and conjunct movement, but only as a last resource. Such a procedure is excessively harsh if the suspension resolve into the third of the chord.

Ex. 66.

In the above examples (c) is better than (a), as the scalic movement of the tenor in short notes justifies the exceptional treatment.

7. The discord must be more strongly accented than its resolution.

Ex. 67.

8. Suspensions do not remove consecutives.

Ex. 68.

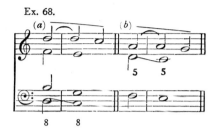

Fifths between upper parts, as in example (*b*), are not bad in effect, but the beginner is advised to use them sparingly.

9. **Suspensions in the bass.** When these are used, no upper part should sound the resolution against the discord.

Ex. 69.

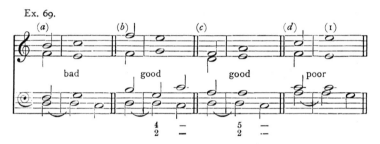

(*d*) is poor, because (1) is not in effect a suspension at all, but the chord of A minor. $\frac{5}{2}\bar{\ }$ and $\frac{4}{2}\bar{\ }$ are the only satisfactory suspensions in the bass, and the former is much the better of the two.

10. The suspended discord may resolve on to another chord, or another position of the same chord.

Ex. 70.

11. Sometimes upward resolving suspensions are used. Only the following are recommended for elementary work:

Ex. 71.

(1) Only use when the seventh is major. The first inversion may be used, as at (d).

(b) should be used rarely. Upward resolving suspensions will be avoided in the bass for the present. (c) may be regarded as two concords. (d), however, is really the first inversion of 7 8 in the minor key.

12. Suspensions may resolve ornamentally,

(a) by leaping to, or taking by step, another factor of the chord of resolution;

(b) by taking the auxiliary note a step below the resolution;

(c) by filling in leaps of thirds in these, with a note producing conjunct movement.

Ex. 72.

13. Double suspensions may be used, moving in thirds or sixths:

Ex. 73.

Triple suspensions move in six-threes:

Ex. 74.

14. Sometimes a complete chord is suspended. But for the satisfactory employment of this no notes should *leap* to the factors of the chord of resolution.

Ex. 75.

15. The combination $\begin{smallmatrix}7&6\\5&6\end{smallmatrix}$ is very useful and satisfactory in effect, whether the 5 be prepared or not.

Ex. 76.

16. In using $\frac{9}{7}\frac{8}{8}$, do not sound 3 against them, as 9 and 7 so strongly indicate a separate chord.

Ex. 77.

poor   good

In the first inversion this is not so.   (See Ex. 76.)

17. In using dominant harmony, the seventh may be used in conjunction with suspensions.   Memorize the following:

Ex. 78.

These combinations are catalogued by some theorists as being separate chords (dominant ninth, eleventh, and thirteenth). Used in the above way, it is much simpler to regard the sounds in question as suspensions. Unprepared, they are appoggiaturas. In using 6 5 with 7, sound 6 5 above 7.

18. Ties may be omitted at discretion.

19. In harmonizing a given part, bear in mind that the normal harmony moves uniformly. Therefore the more irregular the rhythm of a given part, the more necessary it is to find a means of maintaining regularity in harmonic rhythm.

Ex. 79.

&c.

Further, a repeated or tied note weak to strong, if descending subsequently by step, should as a rule be regarded as a suspended discord, especially if a bass.

Ex. 80.

&c.

&c.

20. Suspensions are useful as a means of avoiding bald harmony, and of keeping up movement, specially in intermediate cadences.

Ex. 81.

Exercises.

(1) Prepare and resolve the following suspensions downwards (*4 parts*):

(2) Prepare and resolve the following suspensions **upwards**:

(3) Prepare and resolve the following suspensions on different positions of the same chord, or on different chords:

(4) Ornamentally resolve the following suspensions in various ways:

(5) Prepare and resolve the following double and triple suspensions:

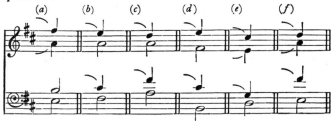

(6) Resolve the following (*a*) as suspensions, (*b*) as appoggiaturas, in each case using a chord to precede the combination:

(7) Add parts for A. and T. to the following cadences:

(g)

(8) Add to the following basses parts for S. A. T.:

(a)

(b)

(9) Harmonize the following for S. A. T. B.:

(a)

(b)

(c)

(10) Add parts for A. and T., introducing some suspensions in these parts; figure the result:

(11) Add parts for S. A. T. in accordance with the figures:

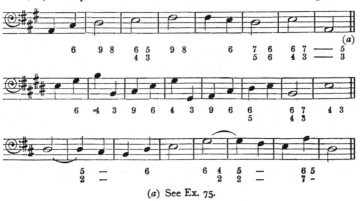

(a) See Ex. 75.

CHAPTER VII

THE CHORD OF THE DOMINANT NINTH

1. IF the diatonic ninth from the root be added to the chord
of the dominant seventh, the resultant combination is called the
chord of the dominant ninth.

Ex. 82.

In the chord of the dominant seventh, the seventh displaces
the root and resolves upon another chord.

Ex. 83.

But the ninth can displace the root or third; and if it displace the root it can resolve while the chord remains, or upon
another harmony. When the ninth resolves while the dominant
harmony remains, it is merely an appoggiatura, or suspension.

Ex. 84.

When the ninth is resolving on to the root, the root should only be sounded against the discord if in the bass.

When resolving on to the third, this factor (the third) should not be sounded against the ninth.

These cases do not require further consideration here, as they are not examples of true chords of the ninth. They are merely embellishments of dominant sevenths. The minor ninth may be thus used in the major key. The major ninth may only be used in the minor key, as at (*a*).

2. When the ninth resolves downwards one step on to a different chord, we get a true chord of the ninth.

Ex. 85.

Here the ninth displaces the root, but resolves on to it with a different harmony.

The major ninth must be sounded above the third. The

minor ninth is used in both major and minor keys, being chromatic in the former. The fifth of the chord is omitted in four parts.

Ex. 86.

3. The dominant ninth may also resolve into a secondary seventh on the sixth degree of the scale (raised in the minor key), if the secondary seventh resolve into a dominant seventh.

Ex. 87.

4. Inversions of the true dominant ninth (e.g. with the root present, and the ninth resolving on to a new chord) are so rare as to be negligible in elementary work.

When the root is absent, the chords are those of the leading seventh and diminished seventh (see Chapter II).

5. The approach of the interval of the ninth by similar motion between extreme parts is poor if when resolving downwards the

substitution of the resolution produces bad exposed octaves, or actual consecutives.

Ex. 88.

poor   good   bad

6. No two parts should proceed in similar motion from 7 to 8 or from 9 to 8.

Ex. 89.

7. The chord of the diminished seventh is derived from the dominant, and is often classified as a dominant minor ninth with the root omitted. It consists of the major third, perfect fifth, minor seventh, and minor ninth from the dominant root. By altering the names of one or more of the sounds forming it, inversions of diminished sevenths in other keys are produced.

Thus, starting with

Ex. 90.
Key C.

B being the third of the root or fundamental, we can make B the fifth of E, the seventh of C sharp, or the ninth (C♭) of B♭.

Ex. 91.

(1) is the 1st inver. of dominant minor ninth in C or C minor.
(2) „ 2nd „ „ „ „ A or A minor.
(3) „ 3rd „ „ „ „ F♯ or F♯ minor.
(4) „ 4th „ „ „ „ E♭ or E♭ minor.
Such changes in notation are called Enharmonic.

This chord can thus be approached as being the dominant diminished seventh of one tonic, and be quitted as that of another producing modulation. The notation of the key approached should be used.

Ex. 92.

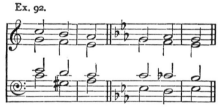

C major to A minor.   C minor to E♭ major.

Modulation to remote keys by this means is not smooth in effect.

8. In referring to dominant ninths the following abbreviations will serve :

(a) dominant major ninth, V_7^9.
(b) „ minor „ $V_7^{♭9}$.

9. Examples 84, 86, and 87 should be used as ear-tests.

10. **Exercises.**

(1) Precede and follow the given chords by other appropriate harmonies, treating the given chords as (a) dominant seventh with suspended root, (b) dominant seventh with appoggiatura of the root, (c) real dominant ninths, resolving directly into new harmony.

(2) Add parts for A. and T.; figure the result:

(3) Harmonize the following, using:

(a) Suspended ninths, (b) appoggiatura ninths, (c) ninths resolving on to different harmony as indicated (a), (b), (c).

(4) Add parts for S. A. T., introducing examples of ninths at the points indicated:

(5) Resolve the following chord in F major:

Making the necessary changes in notation, resolve it in (a) D minor, (b) B minor.

CHAPTER VIII

THE DOMINANT THIRTEENTH

1. THERE is nothing that need be catalogued as a chord of the dominant eleventh. For in using the fourth (eleventh as a compound interval) from the root over a dominant seventh, the fourth must resolve a step upwards or downwards while the rest of the chord remains. It is therefore either a suspension or an appoggiatura:

Ex. 93.　　　　　　　(a)

(a) It would be extremely harsh to sound B against C at (a): hence two appoggiaturas are used. Compare:

Ex. 94.

good

The fourth of the dominant chord may of course decorate the chord of the ninth as well as the seventh, or the plain common chord.

Ex. 95.

2. Just as the eleventh is a temporary displacement of the third, so the thirteenth displaces the fifth. It must not be sounded below the seventh because of the ugly effect.

Ex. 96.

At (*a*) the thirteenth decorates the dominant common chord.
At (*b*) „   „   „   „   „   seventh.
At (*c*) and (*d*) the first and last inversions of the dominant seventh are thus decorated.   The second inversion is rare.

Ex. 97.

This is really VII *b*.

As the chords of the leading and diminished seventh are derivatives of the dominant, it will be convenient to catalogue here a similar decoration of them.

Ex. 98.

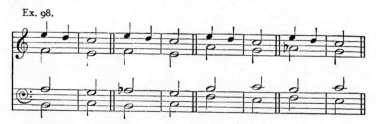

The minor thirteenth can be thus used only in the minor key, and the major thirteenth only in the major key.

3. But the thirteenth becomes a true factor of the chord when the above resolution is omitted, though mentally understood. In this case the thirteenth leaps down direct to the root of the tonic chord, or any chord of which this note is a factor (cf. Pt. I, p. 99).

Ex. 99.

By this principle of elision of resolution this discord may be added to the chords of the leading and diminished seventh (displacing the third from the leading note).

Ex. 100.

4. Sometimes the thirteenth remains to be a part of the next chord :

Ex. 101.

This is intelligible when it is remembered that it is merely a condensation of

Ex. 102.

5. A cnromatic raising of the fifth of the chord is usually catalogued as a thirteenth, being regarded as false notation for the flattened sixth (cf. Pt. I, p. 96).

Ex. 103.

This view obtains some support from the fact that in the minor key the raised fifth would not be written, as it has to remain stationary as the third of the tonic, or else it must fall.

Ex. 104.

Thus it is said that the dominant minor thirteenth can be used in the major key if rising. The particular view taken is immaterial. The exposed octaves at (b) are allowable, because E♮ is merely a displacement of D.

6. The second inversion of the dominant thirteenth is not used, as the thirteenth against the fifth is extremely harsh. The last inversion is not used, as the thirteenth below the seventh is also harsh.

Ex. 105.

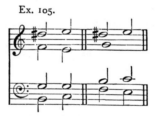

The fourth inversion is only used with the minor ninth. The major ninth should not be sounded below the third.

Ex. 106.

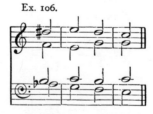

7. The following abbreviations will serve for these chords ·
Dominant major thirteenth V^{13}_{7}.

„   minor   „ $V^{♭13}_{7}$.

or $V^{7}_{♯5}$.

8. The following examples of combined appoggiaturas or suspensions resolving into dominant harmony should be memorized. Alternative analyses are given.

Ex. 107.

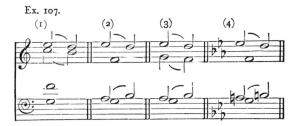

(1) (a) dominant thirteenth with eleventh.

(b) double appoggiaturas or suspensions of fifth and third of dominant seventh.

(2) (a) dominant thirteenth with ninth.

(b) Upward and downward resolving suspensions or appoggiaturas of the third and fifth of dominant seventh.

(3) (a) Incomplete dominant thirteenth with ninth (a true dominant discord should contain the seventh).

(b) Appoggiaturas of the third and fifth of dominant seventh.

(4) As in (2).

9. As the resource discussed is merely a decoration of the dominant common chord and seventh, it will be obvious that the usual place for its employment will be either (a) at the start when it is necessary to establish the key, or (b) at the end of a sentence where a full close is desirable, or (c) at intermediate places where a new key has to be established (a new V to I with I or both V and I in inverted positions).

10. Ear-tests.

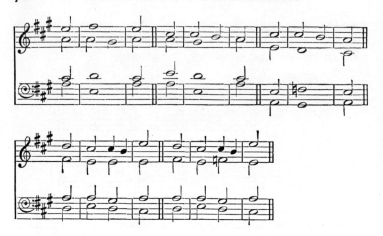

The above should also be transposed into the key of the tonic minor.

Use also examples in paragraph 8.

Exercises.

(1) Precede and follow the given chords by other appropriate harmonies; treat any discords higher than the seventh as suspensions or appoggiaturas.

(2) Precede and follow the given chords by other appropriate harmonies; treat discords higher than the ninth as suspensions or appoggiaturas.

(3) Precede and follow the given chords by other appropriate harmonies, treating them as true chords of the thirteenth.

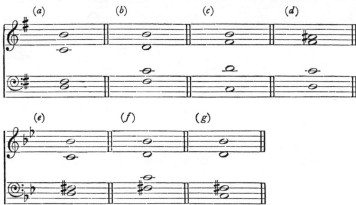

(4) Harmonize the following, introducing the resource discussed in this chapter (S. A. T. B.):

(5) Elaborate the following with the resource discussed in this chapter; alter anything except the bass; and figure the result:

(6) Fill in the harmony where omitted; figure the result:

(7) Harmonize the following basses for S. A. T. B., using the various resource discussed at the points indicated:

(8) Add in the blank spaces chords of the dominant seventh and ninth with appoggiatura of the third resolving:

(see Ex. 95.)

(see Ex. 95.)

(9) Add in the blank spaces chords of the dominant seventh with appoggiatura of the fifth resolving (see Ex. 96):

(10) Add in the blank spaces chords of the leading and

diminished seventh (with third from leading note displaced and resolved while the chord remains); see Ex. 98:

(11) Add true chords of the thirteenth in the blank spaces (see Ex. 99):

(12) Ditto with addition of minor ninth (see Ex. 100):

(13) Write original examples introducing the dominant seventh with sharpened fifth (major keys); see Ex. 103:

(14) Decorate the dominant chords as in Ex. 107:

CHAPTER IX

ADDITIONAL EXERCISES

1. It is advisable to have various types of problems in order to get familiar with the resource of harmony and the different demands made upon the capacity of the student. Further, it is a bad plan to adhere to one type of question.

2. I. **Figured Bass.** (*a*) This is the least useful type of question, as it settles the chord progressions. All therefore that the student can do is to attempt to write a melodious soprano part and correct inner parts. Care should be taken to vary the pitch of the soprano, so as to avoid dullness. The part should rise to at least one climax, and particular care should be taken to make the cadences satisfactory in their arrangement. The cadences at the end of the second and fourth phrases require the effect of finality. Therefore the root of the final chord of the Full Close should as a rule be in the top part. In other cases, where a note is common to the two chords, it should not be repeated in the melody. Exceptions will, of course, occur.

Ex. 108.

Melodic tautology should be avoided.

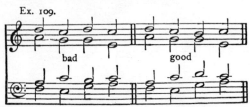

Ex. 109.

(*b*) Similarly, an inelegant part caused **by the** juxtaposition of two notes of the same name, one of them chromatically altered, may be avoided by a redistribution of the parts.

Ex. 110.

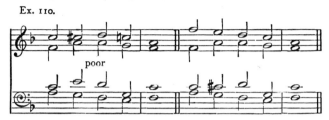

(*c*) As it is an examiner's aim to find out a student's knowledge of chords, he will naturally include chords that require special treatment. In this connexion bear in mind:

(1) Cases in which the seventh in the dominant seventh may rise;

(2) The treatment of diminished and augmented triads in root position;

(3) The dominant major ninth must be sounded above the third unless resolving while the chord remains: it must be sounded above the third in the chord of the leading seventh;

(4) The thirteenth must be sounded above the seventh;

(5) Special treatment of some diatonic sevenths;

(6) The use of the melodic minor scale in harmonization.

(*d*) It is unfortunate that in the system of figuring a formula may mean one thing at one time, and another thing at another. But an examiner seizes on this to test the candidate's knowledge.

(1) 7 generally implies $\frac{7}{5}$. But when followed by a 6 on the same bass note it implies a suspension of the root of a chord.

Ex. 111.

(2) $\frac{4}{2}$ if resolving into a 6 on the note below means $\frac{6}{4}$.

When followed by a note below, with horizontal lines after the figures, it implies a suspension or appoggiatura. When the bass leaps from $\frac{4}{2}$ and does not resolve on the note below, $\frac{4}{2}$ implies two passing notes. $\frac{6}{4}$ in a similar case implies three passing notes.

Ex. 112.

(3) $\frac{6}{4}$ may imply the chord of the $\frac{6}{4}$ or two unessential notes, or the incomplete dominant thirteenth, or a retardation.

Ex. 113.

Such figuring as the following may trap the unwary :

Ex. 114.

good   bad

(e) Sometimes the essential figuring only is given and students are required to put in their own unessential notes— passing and auxiliary notes, appoggiaturas, suspensions, &c. Care must be taken to obtain a fair distribution of them between the parts, and not to overload any single part with them.

Ex. 115.

If the bass give any indication of any figure, it is better to try to use it in the added parts.

Ex. 116.

But care must be taken to vary it and give it a rest, to prevent its degenerating into a tag.

(*f*) In all problems in music always look ahead. If the bass move up to a high note, the soprano should usually come down to meet it, or at any rate get into position so as to avoid overlapping.

Ex. 117.

(*g*) Whether the bass be figured or not, the student should see if it contains any sequential passages. If so, the soprano at any rate should also be sequential in conjunction with the bass.

Further, if the bass of two phrases starts or ends in a similar manner, it is intended that the soprano should likewise exhibit statement and response.

Ex. 118.

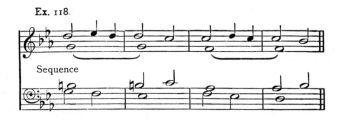

Beginning of first phrase :

Beginning of a later phrase :

Ending of one phrase :

Ending of another :

It is often quite good to introduce in the response some little variation from the original statement. But there is no harm in the exact reproduction of a section either in the same or a new key in the course of the problem.

3. II. **Unfigured Bass.** This leaves the choice of harmony to the student, and demands also the formation of a good **melody**. The various points to be remembered have already **been** discussed under other headings.

Two common faults should be specially noted :

(*a*) If the bass have a repeated or tied note weak to strong, the note on the strong accent must not be treated as a concord, but as a discord, if moving one step downwards.

Ex. 119.

(*b*) Beware of using a six-four on the strong accent, unless resolving into a $\frac{5}{3}$ or its equivalent.

Ex. 120.

4. III. **Harmonization of Melodies.** This tests the sense of harmonic progression, and the power of forming a good bass. The student should look up Chapter V. Many of the points mentioned there are applicable. Add:

(*a*) A repeated or tied note weak to strong should have the harmony changed on the strong beat. At a cadence this is vital.

Ex. 121.

(*b*) If the repeated note fall one degree, direct or ornamentally, it is usually a suspension.

Ex. 122.

(*c*) If a melody is sequential, aim at reproducing the sequence in the added parts.

Ex. 123.

(*d*) Be careful to lead up to the bass of the cadences, thus avoiding anticipating them.

5. IV. **Given inner part.** As this type of problem is more difficult, only the easiest exercises will be given. To this inner part the remaining three parts must be added. This tests at one and the same time the power to construct a good soprano and bass. The given part is the alto or tenor of a simple chord progression with the addition of a few unessential notes. The student should first of all settle the cadences and modulations, then add the bass, and finally the remaining parts. He must never allow himself to write dull harmony or a poor melody because of the uninteresting nature of the given middle part.

An example of the type of work is given in the Exercises.

6. V. **Writing a sentence introducing given chords or combinations.**

This type of question tests the knowledge of the treatment of various chords, and the ability to use them in a musical way.

(*a*) Note if any chords are specially suitable for cadences, and reserve them for these points. For example, the six-four on the dominant, or a suspension of the dominant chord over the tonic note.

Ex. 124.

(*b*) If any chords foreign to the tonic key are given, make the necessary modulations at the right places. If the chord of B flat were given in a problem commencing and ending in C major, the chord would occur in the key of F towards the end.

(*c*) Be careful to resolve all discords properly.

For an example, see pp. 95, 96.

7. VI. **Writing a sentence introducing prescribed modula·
tions.**

Look up Chapters IV and V.

Aim at some imitation in the phrases.

If there are two phrases, it is well to attempt to make their openings correspond.

If there are four phrases, the second or fourth, or both, may imitate the first in their openings, and the fourth may imitate the cadence of the second. The third phrase usually subdivides into two smaller sections, and a corresponding portion of the first phrase may be imitated.

8. VII. **Ground Bass.** This is a bass repeated a few times but varied in treatment each time. At the present stage nothing but the most elementary treatment will be required.

Plan :

(1) State the bass alone.

(2) First repetition harmonized with plain chords and a few unessential notes.

(3) Second repetition harmonized with suspensions as charac·
teristic feature.

(4) Third repetition harmonized with passing and auxiliary notes ; end with tonic chord.

In the first harmonization of the bass, establish the tonic ; in the second and third repetitions use appropriate modulation, first to the sharp side or relative key, and then to the flat side.

9. Examples.

Figured bass.

Ex. 125.

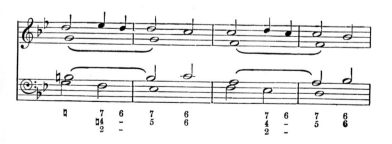

Unfigured bass.

Ex. 126.

Melody harmonized.
Ex. 127.

(a) It is common to avoid a Full Close in the tonic by following the dominant by the dominant of the relative minor.

Any of the three previous examples (Ex. 125, 126, and 127) could be the result of any one of the three types of question illustrated. Ex. 125 might have been an unfigured bass or a melody. Ex. 126 might have been a melody or figured bass. And Ex. 127 might have been a figured or unfigured bass.

10. Similarly, any of them might have resulted from the setting of the alto or tenor as the given part.

11. Again, Ex. 125 might have resulted from the following form of question: Begin as follows (bars 1-4 given) and modulate to D minor, C minor, B flat major, and back to G minor. The others could be re-stated in the same way.

12. Finally, they could all be the result of a question in this form: Write sixteen bars beginning and ending in the tonic key, introducing the following chords in any order appropriate, and making the necessary modulations. Ex. 127 would be the result of such a question, beginning and ending in F major, and introducing the following chords:

Ex. 128.

The chords may be introduced in any order, and in any time value, but with exact arrangement given.

It will thus be seen that all the above questions are merely tests in different aspects of the same thing. The result in each case must be a piece of intelligible music.

Ground Bass.

Ex. 129.

This working has been purposely made very simple and innocuous. It is sufficient at this elementary stage for the student to use his material correctly. Really musical students would probably produce something much more artistic. It is given as an example of what may be expected from the average student.

Exercises.

(1) Add parts for S. A. T. in accordance with the figures:

This period contains twelve bars. There is no necessity to maintain a rigid pattern of sixteen bars. In fact variety is desirable.

(2) Add parts for S. A. T. in accordance with the figures:

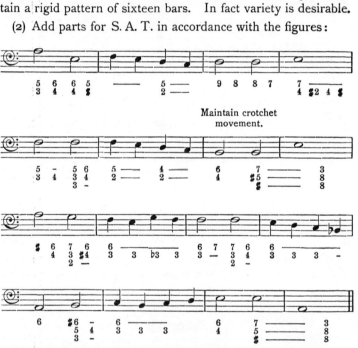

(3) Add parts for S. A. T. to the following unfigured Basses:

(a)

(b)

(c) Maintain crotchet movement.

(1)

(1)

(1) When a tied bass note has been retained for the whole of the previous bar, the note on the succeeding strong accent need not be treated as a discord.

(d)

(4) Harmonize the following melodies for S. A. T. B.:

(1) Maintain crotchet movement.

(5) Add the remaining parts to the following, producing plain chord progressions with a few unessential notes:

(a) Alto. (See foot-note *.)

(1) Change the chord on the accent, and regard F as a suspension.

(b) Alto.

(c) Alto.   through C minor.

(d) Alto.   to A minor.

(e) Alto.

* Example of type of result required:
Tenor part given.

(6) Write eight-bar sentences, divided into two phrases of four bars each, introducing the following chords:

(a) Key C major (no modulation). (See foot-note*.)

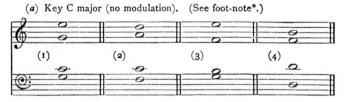

* Example of type of result required. (Numbered chords given.)

(*b*) Key G major (no modulation).

(*c*) Key F major (no modulation).

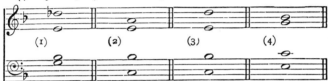

(*d*) Key D minor (no modulation).

(*e*) Key A major (with modulation).

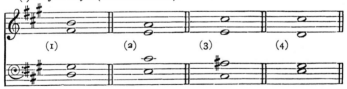

(*f*) B♮ major (with modulation).

(*g*) Key C major (with modulation).

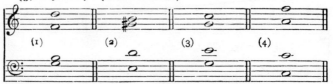

(7) Begin as follows, and in eight bars (two phrases):

(*a*) Modulate to A minor and back to C.

(*b*) Modulate to D minor and back to C (same start).

(*c*) Modulate to F major and back to C (same start).

(8) Begin as follows, and in eight bars (two phrases):

(*a*) Modulate to C major and back to A minor.

(*b*) Modulate to F major and back to A minor (same start).

(*c*) Modulate to E minor and back to A minor (same start).

(9) Begin as follows:

and proceed thus:

> Bars 5-8, responsive phrase through B minor to Full Close in
>   A major.
> „ 9-10, sub-phrase, modulation to G major.
> „ 11-12,   „   „   E minor.
> „ 13-16, back to D major.

(10) Begin as follows:

> Bars 5-8, responsive phrase through F major to C major.
> „ 9-10, sub-phrase, modulation to B flat major.
> „ 11-12,   „   „   G minor.
> „ 13-16, back to D minor.

(11) Ground Basses (three repetitions in each case, in addition
to the statement):

(a)

(b)

(c)

(d)

(e)

(12) Add parts for S. A. T., introducing unessential notes:

(a)

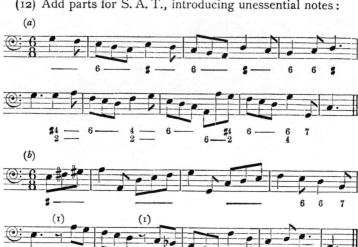

(b)

(1) Let the upper parts move on the accents.

(c)

(2) Maintain crotchet movement over semibreves in some part, and imitate the bass of the succeeding bar. Crotchet movement should be fairly continuous throughout.

ELEMENTARY HARMONY

HARMONY

PART III

BY

C. H. KITSON

M.A. Cantab., D.Mus. Oxon

PROFESSOR OF MUSIC, UNIVERSITY COLLEGE, DUBLIN
SENIOR PROFESSOR OF THEORY, ROYAL IRISH
ACADEMY OF MUSIC, DUBLIN

OXFORD   NEW YORK
OXFORD UNIVERSITY PRESS

PREFACE

THIS part concludes the elementary survey of Harmony as practised up to the time of Brahms. The student, of course, knows that this technique is now practically a dead language. But there are two valid reasons for still teaching it: (1) The new technique is not yet sufficiently settled for the formation of any systematized theory; (2) Students ought to understand the technique of the various periods. Broadly, we now have three periods:

(1) The Polyphonic Period—up to 1600; this technique is or should be studied under the heading of Strict Counterpoint.

(2) The Homophonic Period, from 1600 up to Brahms.

(3) The Modern 'New Music', as seen in the works of Debussy, Ravel, Scriabin, Delius, Schönberg, &c.

In the Polyphonic Period the contrapuntal aspect of music is chiefly revealed, for the simple reason that combined sound itself was the result of combined melodies. In later periods we have both the harmonic and the contrapuntal styles, and the second is always the later manifestation. For, obviously, a writer cannot give attention to the individuality of his various parts till he is thoroughly conversant with the harmonic basis underlying their combination.

This book has dealt with the purely harmonic side of the period. The student's next step is to study the contrapuntal phase.

It may further be urged that the best-equipped person for attempting modern technique is he who understands the whole process of development.

C. H. KITSON.

CONTENTS

CHAPTER I

CHAPTER I

CHROMATIC SUPERTONIC COMMON CHORD AND SEVENTH

1. ONE of the best approaches to Cadences (except the Plagal) is obtained by employing Chord II *a* or *b*.

Ex. 1.

By sharpening the third in Chord II, a new colour is added to the resource of harmony.

Ex. 2.

This chord is derived from the dominant key, being the dominant of the dominant. Its natural tendency is to lead into its own tonic, and thus to produce a modulation to the dominant.

Ex. 3.

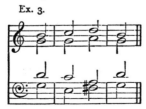

If it be desired to prevent modulation, the chord must be followed by the tonic common chord or the dominant seventh. In the latter case the chromatic note usually falls a chromatic semitone (see Example 2 (*b*)). But the following is also common :

Ex. 4.

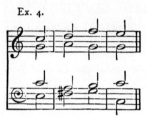

2. If the seventh be added to the chord, a fundamental seventh precisely like the dominant seventh is formed. It is in fact the dominant seventh of the dominant key.

The resolutions are as follows :

(*a*) On to the dominant seventh.

Ex. 5.

The seventh in the supertonic chord may rise to the fifth in the dominant chord, if the fifth in the former rise to the third in the latter.

Ex. 6.

(*b*) On to the second inversion of the tonic chord, which will itself resolve into the dominant seventh.

In this case the seventh of the supertonic will remain to be a part of the tonic chord, and it is better that it should then fall.

Ex. 7.

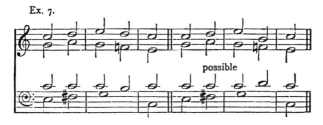

Or it may rise to the third of the tonic chord as the fifth rises to the root.

Ex. 8.

This is merely a decoration of Ex. 6.

In these cases the supertonic seventh really resolves on to the dominant seventh, as the six-four of the tonic is merely an appoggiatura chord. But inasmuch as it gives the effect of a cadence in the tonic, the addition of the seventh to the dominant chord is unnecessary.

Ex. 9.

The major third in the supertonic seventh must not be doubled, because of its fixed movement and 'leading' character.

3. As VII*b* of the dominant key is really the incomplete supertonic seventh, it may be added here:

Ex. 10.

4. The supertonic chromatic common chord and seventh may also be used in the minor key.

Ex. 11.

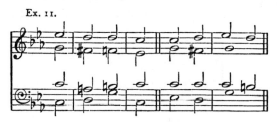

But care must be taken to avoid the melodic interval of the augmented second, as for example E♭ to F♯ in C minor.

5. This chord may be decorated by appoggiatura or suspension.

(*a*) Root decorated:

Ex. 12.

The minor ninth may be used in the major or minor key; but not the major ninth in the minor key.

* Note the chord of the *seventh* may be used in any inversion.

(*b*) Third, or root and third decorated:

Ex. 13.

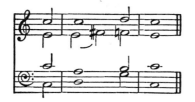

(*c*) Fifth, or fifth and third decorated:

Ex. 14.

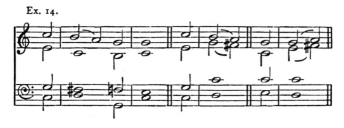

In the minor key the decoration of the fifth by the sixth is impracticable.

Ex. 15.

For the same reason, the use of the minor sixth of the root as a decoration in the major key should be avoided.

6. Note that the resource discussed is best used as an approach to any cadence except the plagal, or as a means of modulation to the dominant key.   Use the examples as ear-tests.

7. Abbreviations for these chords :
Supertonic Chromatic Triad, II ($\sharp$3).

„   „   Seventh, $\overset{\text{II}}{\underset{\sharp 3}{7}}$ (or $\natural$ 3, as the case may be).

Exercises.

(1) Harmonize the following, introducing the chromatic supertonic common chord (cadences and their approach) :

(2) Resolve the following chords in D major and D minor, adding the proper key-signatures :

(3) Resolve the following in three different ways:

(See Ex. 5, 6 and 8.)

(4) Add parts for alto and tenor. Treat the notes over which slurs are placed as decorated forms of the supertonic seventh:

(5) At the points marked × substitute double suspensions, or appoggiaturas:

par. 5 (b)   par. 5 (c)

(6) Add parts for S. A. T. to the following unfigured basses:

(a)

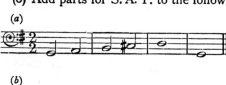

(b)

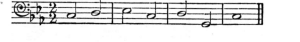

(c)

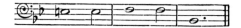

(7) Harmonize the following for S. A. T. B.:

(a)

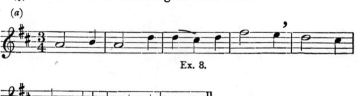

Ex. 8.

Ex. 13.

(b)

Ex. 13.

Ex. 12.

(c)

(8) Add parts for A. and T. in accordance with the figures, introducing some unessential notes (the soprano may be elaborated):

CHAPTER II

CHROMATIC SUPERTONIC NINTH
AND THIRTEENTH

1. THE major or minor ninth in the supertonic discord may be used as an essential harmony note, without preparation.

The major or minor ninth can be used in the major key; only the minor ninth in the minor key.

(*a*) The major ninth either falls one degree into the dominant seventh:

Ex. 16.

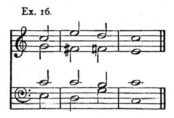

or remains to be the third of the tonic chord, or thirteenth of the dominant:

Ex. 17.

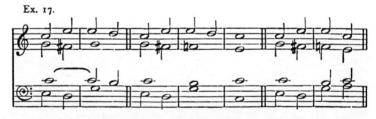

(*b*) The minor ninth in the minor key is treated in the same way. Transpose the above examples into C minor.

(*c*) The minor ninth in the major key either falls to the fifth of the dominant or rises a chromatic semitone to the third of the tonic.

Ex. 18.

In the latter case (a) the minor ninth is often written as the sharpened root (D♯).

2. In the inversions the root is generally omitted, and the chords are the Leading and Diminished Sevenths of the dominant key.

Ex. 19.

The major ninth must be sounded above the third, hence the last inversion of the supertonic major ninth is not used. In this chord the only really free note is the fifth from the fundamental.

3. Note the use of the diminished seventh of the dominant key as a link between two statements of the tonic chord in root position or first inversion:

Ex. 20.

Another explanation of the combinations at (a) and (b) is that they are auxiliary notes.

4. Consecutive chords of the diminished seventh may be used.

Ex. 21.

At (a) the seventh of the dominant rises a chromatic semitone.

5. The only supertonic thirteenth that need be considered is the major form. It is in any case rare. It must resolve into the dominant seventh.

Ex. 22.

6. Chromatic supertonic harmony is very useful for purposes of modulation.   It forms a strong approach to the new key, and should generally be used as supertonic in reference to the new key.

(*a*) Any diatonic major common chord can be quitted as a chromatic supertonic common chord in a new key.

Key C major.

I quitted as Chromatic II in B♭ major or minor.
IV   „   „   E♭ major or minor.
V   „   „   F major or minor.

Key C minor.

V quitted as Chromatic II in F major or minor.
VI   „   „   G♭ major or minor.

Ex. 23.

```
            V  C major ⎫              I  C  major ⎫
            Ch. II F major ⎭          Ch. II B♭ major ⎭
```

(*b*) The dominant seventh or ninth can be quitted as a supertonic seventh or ninth of a new key.

Ex. 24.

```
         V 7 C major ⎫              V 9 G major ⎫
         Ch. II 7 F major ⎭         Ch. II 9 C major ⎭
```

(*c*) The chord of the diminished seventh of the supertonic will obviously be a very fruitful means of modulation, because of its enharmonic possibilities.

We may, of course, approach a fundamental discord as being supertonic in one key and leave it as dominant in another. It is better to approach as dominant, and leave as supertonic. But the diminished seventh by enharmonic change can be supertonic of the key quitted and also of the key approached. Use the notation of the latter. A few illustrations will make these points clear:

Ex. 25.

Ch. II 9 C major ⎫   V 9 C major ⎫
V 9 G major ⎬   Ch. II 9 F major ⎬

C major   A minor

II 9 C major (D♯ = E♭), Root D.
II 9 A minor, Root B.

The enharmonic changes of the supertonic diminished seventh are:

Ex. 26.

Root D   Root B   Root G♯   Root A♭   Root F

The correct notation can easily be found by remembering that the sounds from the fundamental are: major third, perfect fifth, minor seventh, and minor ninth. Also bear in mind that the harmonic chromatic scale has the following notation : tonic and dominant once, the rest twice.

Ex. 27.

C major or minor.

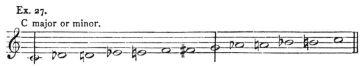

The theoretical notation of these discords follows the scale of the key used.

Use the examples as ear-tests.

7. Abbreviations if required :

$$\text{II}\,{}^{9}_{7.}\!{}_{\sharp} \qquad\qquad \text{II}\,{}^{7}_{6.}\!{}_{\sharp}$$

8. **Compound Modulation.** A series of fundamental sevenths with roots falling a fifth in succession may be used. In this case no key is confirmed till a concord is used in cadential idiom.

Ex. 28.

V 7 C ⎱ V 7 F ⎱ V 7 B♭ ⎱ V 7 E♭ ⎱ V 7 A♭ ⎱ V D♭   I D♭
II 7 F ⎰ II 7 B♭ ⎰ II 7 E♭ ⎰ II 7 A♭ ⎰ II 7 D♭ ⎰

Exercises.

(1) Give various resolutions of the following chords :

(a)   (b)   (c)

(2) Resolve the following chords in the key of D **major**:

(3) Place a supertonic diminished seventh between the following chords:

(4) Follow each of the following by **a** different diminished seventh, and resolve the latter:

(5) In four chords modulate:

　(*a*) from D major to G major by means of a supertonic chromatic common chord in G major.

　(*b*) from D major to C major by means of a supertonic chromatic common chord in C major.

　(*c*) from D major to G major by means of a supertonic chromatic seventh in G major.

　(*d*) from D major to G **major** by means of a supertonic chromatic ninth in G major.

(6) Write the following chord with the correct notation for the keys specified, and state whether it is dominant or supertonic:

(a) Key D major.	(e) Key A major.
(b) „ B major.	(f) „ F♯ minor.
(c) „ A♭ major.	(g) „ E♭ major.
(d) „ F major.	(h) „ C major.

Resolve the chord in all these keys.

(7) Harmonize the following fragments, introducing the super-tonic ninth or diminished seventh:

(8) Add parts for S. A. T. to the following basses, introducing supertonic chromatic discords :

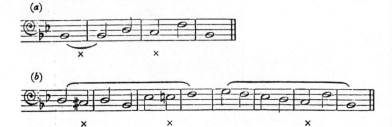

(9) Harmonize the following for S. A. T. B. :

(10) Add parts for S. A. T. (introduce some unessential notes) ; maintain crotchet movement as a general feature :

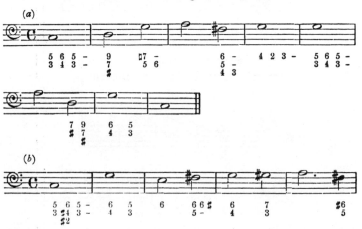

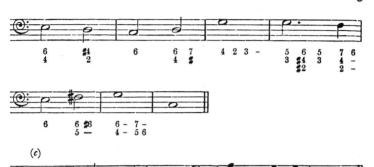

CHAPTER III

CHROMATIC TONIC DISCORDS

1. This chapter is concerned with the fundamental discords derived from the dominant of the lower dominant or subdominant. These are termed Tonic Discords.

The following example gives the complete series of dominant, supertonic, and tonic discords:

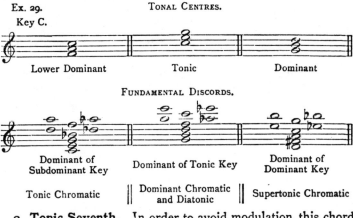

Ex. 29.
Key C.

TONAL CENTRES.

Lower Dominant   Tonic   Dominant

FUNDAMENTAL DISCORDS.

Dominant of Subdominant Key   Dominant of Tonic Key   Dominant of Dominant Key

Tonic Chromatic || Dominant Chromatic and Diatonic || Supertonic Chromatic

2. **Tonic Seventh.** In order to avoid modulation, this chord must be followed by:

(a) A dominant discord, the seventh of the tonic rising a chromatic semitone:

Ex. 30.
Key C.

or (*b*) a supertonic discord, the latter proceeding as explained in the previous chapters.

Ex. 31.

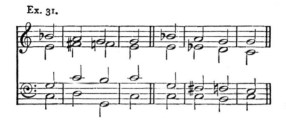

The third of the chord must not be doubled.   It may rise a tone or semitone or fall a chromatic semitone.

It will thus be seen that (*a*) supertonic discords resolve into tonic concords or dominant discords, (*b*) tonic discords resolve into dominant or supertonic discords, if modulation is to be averted.

The use of the tonic discord in the minor key is rarer than in the major key, because it requires a chromatic alteration of the third.

3. The tonic seventh is best used for the purpose of modulation, being quitted as a dominant or supertonic seventh.

Ex. 32.

Or it may be approached as a dominant or supertonic and quitted as tonic, producing an abrupt modulation.

Ex. 33

V 7 F major }
I 7 C major }

II 7 Bb }
I 7 C major }

4. The chord may be decorated by suspension or appoggiatura:

(*a*) decoration of root, by major or minor ninth in major or minor key:

Ex. 34.

(*b*) decoration of third, or root and third:

Ex. 35.

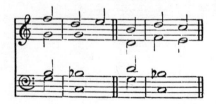

(*c*) decoration of fifth, or fifth and third :

Ex. 36.

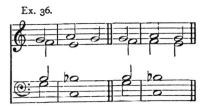

The major sixth may only decorate the fifth in the major key.
The minor sixth may decorate the fifth in both major and minor
keys.

5. **Tonic Ninth.** The ninth may be major or minor in either
the major or minor key.

The resolutions of the chord are, of course, the same as those
of the tonic seventh.

The ninth may (*a*) remain to be a part of the next chord,
(*b*) fall one degree, (*c*) if minor rise a chromatic semitone.

Ex. 37. Key C.

The diminished seventh of the tonic fundamental is best used
as a decoration of the dominant.

Ex. 38.

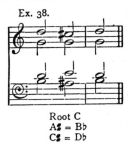

Root C
A♯ = B♭
C♯ = D♭

Thus the supertonic diminished seventh decorates tonic chord.

  „   tonic   „   „   „   dominant „

Ex. 39.

These harmonies should be very sparingly used.

6. Tonic Thirteenth.

(*a*) The resolutions are the same as those of the tonic seventh.

(*b*) The major or minor thirteenth may be used in the major key; only the minor thirteenth in the minor key.

(*c*) The major and minor thirteenths either remain to be a part of the next chord, or fall one degree. The minor thirteenth may rise a chromatic semitone.

Ex. 40.

G♯ = A♭

The examples should be used as ear-tests.

Abbreviations if required:

      Tonic seventh: I ♭7 (or ♮, as the case may be).

         „   ninth: I ♭$\frac{9}{7}$.

         „   thirteenth: I ♭$\frac{7}{6}$.

Exercises.

(1) Resolve the following chord in two ways without modulation, adding a few chords to form a cadence:

(2) By means of the above chord, modulate
   (a) from D major to G minor ;
   (b) „   D major „ C major ;
   (c) „   G major „ D major ;
   (d) „   C major „ D major.

(3) Decorate the fundamental sevenths in the following, by suspension or appoggiatura :

(4) Precede and resolve the following chords in E major, adding a few more chords to form cadences :

(5) Add parts for A. and T.:

(6) Harmonize the following for S. A. T. B.:

(a)

(b)

(7) Harmonize the following unfigured basses for S. A. T. B.:

(a)

(*b*)

(8) Add parts for S. A. T., introducing unessential notes:

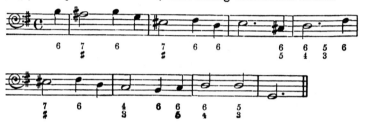

CHAPTER IV

CHIEF CHROMATIC TRIADS

1. The following is a list of the generally accepted chromatic triads of the major and minor keys:

Ex. 41.
Key C major. Major series.

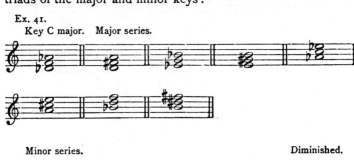

Minor series.   Diminished.

Key C minor.

Only the chief of them will be considered, and their best uses.

2. In the following examples:

Ex. 42.
(a)

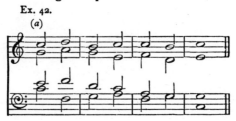

note at (*a*) a series of diatonic chords in C major;

at (*b*) the corresponding diatonic series in C minor;

at (*c*) some of the chords from the minor key incorporated in a passage in C major without producing modulation.

(*c*) only differs from (*b*) in the first and last chords, but it is in C major, not in C minor.

Note in (*c*) a new form of the False Cadence in the major key (at *d*).

3. Care must be taken not to follow I by IV (♭ 3), else a modulation to the subdominant minor is produced, unless of course such modulation be desired. But at the very outset of a piece, this does not matter. The modulation is only theoretical.

Ex. 43.

IV (♭ 3) is often used as a variation of the diatonic plagal cadence.

But beware of such bad taste as the following:

4. The chromatic triad on the minor second of the scale is commonly used in its first inversion as an approach to the half or perfect cadence in both major and minor keys.

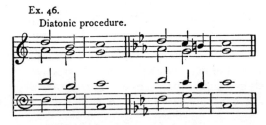

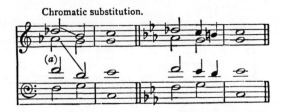

Note at (*a*) the melodic interval of the diminished third (D♭ to B♮), and the permissible False Relation D♭, D♮. The third of the chord should be doubled. This chord in the first inversion is known as the Neapolitan sixth.

The chord is rare in its root position, except as a means of modulation.

Ex. 47.

&c.

♭II C major.
VI F minor.

5. The simplest use of many of these chords is to employ them as auxiliary chords of the adjacent diatonic chords (a semitone apart).

Ex. 48.

&c.

6. Another good use is to approach them as chromatic in the first key and quit them as diatonic in a new key.

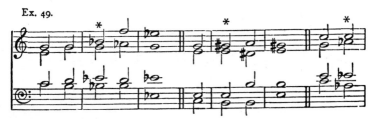

Ex. 49.

They can, of course, be approached as diatonic in the first key and quitted as chromatic in the second key.

Ex. 50.

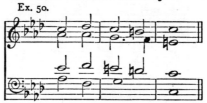

Or they can be approached as chromatic in the first key and quitted as chromatic in the second key.

Ex. 51.   (a)

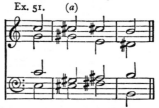

The chord at (a) is the Neapolitan sixth in C major (chord of D♭) and is quitted as the supertonic chromatic triad in B major.

7. If, however, for the sake of practice it be desired to approach them and quit them in the same key it is best to precede and follow them by some diatonic chord a semitone above or below, or by some diatonic chord having a note in common, but not inducing modulation.

Ex. 52.

But such examples as these are not given for imitation.

8. If a modulation to a key whose relationship is remote be required, it is often best to do it by using a chromatic chord as the beginning of a new phrase, and then treating it as diatonic in the new key.

For example, suppose the following to be a given start in C major:

Ex. 53.

and also that by bar 8 a Full Close in G major be required, followed by a modulation to E♭ major. It would be advisable to start the new phrase with the chord of E♭, and imitate the opening bars.

Ex. 54.

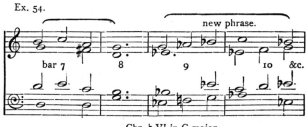

Chr. ♭ VI in G major.
Diatonic I in E♭ major.

9. The minor common chord on the tonic in the major key had better be left alone in elementary work.

10. It will be observed that the chords of E major, A major, and B major (as used in C major) contain notes foreign to the harmonic chromatic scale of C major. That simply means that the notation of this scale is inadequate to explain all the resource of a key. For elementary work, however, it serves its purpose well.

Exercises.

(1) Write the following passage in D minor, then again in D major with some of the chords of the minor key retained:

(2) Re-write the following passage, with chromatic chords substituted for those marked ×:

(3) Re-write the following cadences, introducing the Neapolitan sixth:

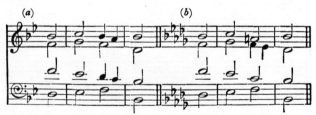

(4) Introduce auxiliary chromatic chords between two statements of the following chords:

(5) By means of chords chromatic in the key quitted, diatonic in the key approached, modulate :

    (*a*) from D major to F major ;

    (*b*)   ,,   ,,   F♯ major ;

    (*c*)   ,,   ,,   B♭ major ;

    (*d*)   ,,   ,,   B major.

(6) By means of the Neapolitan sixth (in the new key), modulate from (*a*) E♭ major to D minor ; (*b*) F major to C major.

(7) Harmonize the following fragments, involving modulation :

(8) Add parts for A. and T.; figure the bass.   Explain the modulations:

(*a*) *Tasto Solo* = leave the bass unharmonized.

CHAPTER V

CHORDS OF THE AUGMENTED SIXTH

1. In the following examples three variants of the second inversion of a supertonic fundamental discord are given:

Ex. 55.
Key C major or minor.

(a) is the incomplete supertonic seventh;
(b) is the complete   ,,   ,,
(c) is the supertonic diminished seventh,
the fundamental of each being D.

A is the fifth of the fundamental; if it is flattened, the chords are called augmented sixths, as A♭ to F♯ forms the interval of an augmented sixth.

Ex. 56.

(d) is termed the Italian sixth;
(e)   ,,   ,,   French   ,.
(f)   ,,   ,,   German   ,,

These chords resolve into either tonic or dominant harmony, thus:

Ex. 57.

At (1) the consecutive fifths are unobjectionable, and are now commonly used. Formerly they were forbidden.

2. As the A♭ is a substitution for A♮, they can both be used while the other factors of the chord remain.

Ex. 58.

(a)   (b)

In case (b), where the augmented sixth rises to its normal note A♮, theorists state that the F♯ can then fall a chromatic semitone; or when the A♭ remains to be the ninth of the dominant fundamental.

Ex. 59.

But here A♭ is merely a suspension, and if this procedure be allowed, the following cannot logically be regarded as incorrect ·

Ex. 60.

However, it is more usual for the sounds forming the augmented sixth to proceed outwards.

3. The chord is commonly used in approaching the Half or Full Close.

Ex. 61.

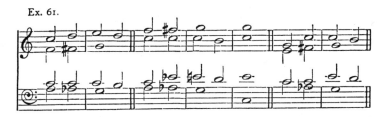

The German sixth is specially useful as a means of modulation. For example, in modulating from A♭ major to C major it can be approached as tonic seventh (A♭, C, E♭, G♭) in A♭, and quitted as German sixth in C major.

Ex. 62.

It can also be approached as supertonic seventh in G♭, and quitted as German sixth in C major.

Ex. 63.

Or it can be approached as dominant seventh in D♮ and quitted as German sixth in C major.

Ex. 64.

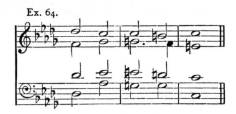

Conversely, a German sixth in the first key can be quitted as tonic, supertonic, or dominant seventh in a new key.

These modulations are both chromatic and enharmonic.

4. A similar series of chords of the augmented sixth is used as a variation of dominant harmony.

Ex. 65.
Key C major.

(*a*) is the incomplete second inversion of the dominant seventh;

(*b*) is the complete   „   „   „   „

(*c*) „ diminished seventh,
the fundamental of each being G.

Flattening the fifth (D)

   (*d*) is termed the Italian sixth ;

   (*e*)   ,,   ,,   French ,,

   (*f*)   ,,   ,,   German ,,

These chords resolve into tonic harmony.

Ex. 66.

(1) is useful as a cadence.

5. The examples should be used as ear-tests.

Exercises.

(1) By chromatic alteration of the bass turn the following into chords of the augmented sixth. State which particular forms they are, and resolve them:

(2) Introduce chords of the augmented sixth in the blank spaces:

(3) Harmonize the following fragments, introducing the chord of the augmented sixth:

(4) Modulate from—

(a) B♭ major to D minor (by means of the German sixth in second key);

(b) A♭ major to D major   ,,   ,,   ,,

(c) E♭ major to D major   ,,   ,,   ,,

(d) C to D♭ major (by means of the German sixth in the first key);

(e) C to G♭ major   ,,   ,,   ,,   ,,

(5) Add parts for A. and T.; figure the bass:

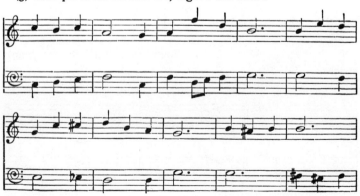

(6) Add parts for S. A. T., with unessential notes:

(a)

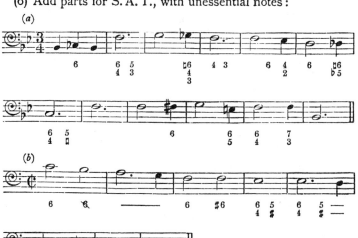

(b)

CHAPTER VI

PEDALS

1. WHEN one part sustains a note while the others proceed with harmony of which it may or may not be a factor, such note is termed a pedal.

Pedals, or pedal points, are generally used in the bass. When used in upper parts they are said to be inverted.

The first and last chords over or under a pedal must in elementary work be chords of which the pedal is a factor.

2. **Bass pedal.**

(*a*) The bass of the first chord must be the root or fifth (in elementary work).

(*b*) The pedal should only be the dominant or tonic note of the key.

(*c*) The pedal should start on the first beat of the bar.

(*d*) The part next above the pedal is to be regarded as the real bass, and it must proceed in accordance with the rules for a bass part, except when the pedal is the root, third, or fifth of any chord used.

Ex. 67.

At (*a*) the fifth of the root is approached by leap from an inversion of another chord, but the pedal is the root itself.

3. Modulations are effective over a pedal. A return to the tonic key should be made before the pedal is quitted.

The following are good modulations:

I. *On dominant pedal in major key.*
    (*a*) Supertonic minor.
    (*b*) Tonic minor.
    (*c*) Subdominant major or minor.
    (*d*) Dominant major.
    (*e*) Submediant minor.

II. *On dominant pedal in minor key.*
    (*a*) Tonic major.
    (*b*) Subdominant minor.
    (*c*) Dominant major or minor.

III. *On tonic pedal in major key.*
    (*a*) Supertonic minor.
    (*b*) Subdominant major or minor.
    (*c*) Relative minor.

IV. *On tonic pedal in minor key.*
    Subdominant minor.

Examples of these are given below.

Ex. 68.

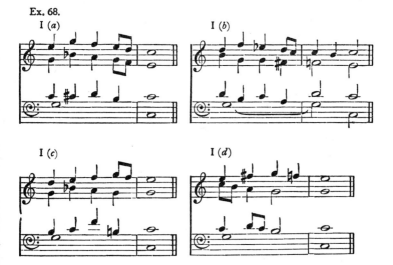

4. A pedal may, of course, contain any number of **modulations**.

Ex. 69.

5. Miniature pedals are used as follows :

(*a*) in commencing a melody.

Ex. 70.

In this case modulation would be injudicious.

(*b*) on the bass of a Half Close.

Ex. 71.

(*c*) in the penultimate bar of the Full Close.
See Ex. 68, I (*a*), (*c*), (*e*).

(*d*) as a plagal extension of the Full Close.

Ex. 72.

Here the modulation to the subdominant is not followed by a modulation back to the tonic, as another Full Close in the tonic would be redundant.

6. Extended dominant pedals are used:

(*a*) as an approach to the Recapitulation in Ternary Form;

(*b*) as an extension of the last phrase;

(*c*) as the coda of such things as Canons and Ground Basses.

The extended tonic pedal is also used in case (*c*), or the coda may be formed on a dominant followed by a tonic pedal.

7. **Inverted pedals.** These will be confined to tonic and dominant in this chapter.

An inverted pedal will not stand much harmony of which it is not a factor.

The following is too harsh for use:

Ex. 73.

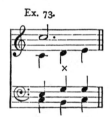

Combinations of which the pedal is not a part should be treated as if they were unessential notes.

Ex. 74.

Inverted pedals are used:

(*a*) at the start of a melody.

Ex. 75.

&c.

(*b*) at the point of recapitulation in the top part, where it is desired to give the actual repetition to another part.

Ex. 76.
Opening.

Recapitulation.

It will be noted that the inverted pedal need not start on the strong accent.

(*c*) at the end of a melody (coda).

Ex. 77.

8. Two parts may use the same pedal at the same time.

Or two parts may combine the tonic and dominant pedal, the tonic being in the bass. This is termed a double pedal.

Exercises.

(1) Add parts for S. A. T. as the first phrase of a sentence:

(*a*) Modulate to the dominant on the pedal.

(2) Add parts for S. A. T. as the first phrase of a sentence:

(3) Add parts for A. T. as the end of a sentence:

(4) Harmonize for S. A. T. B. as the start of a piece:

(5) Taking (a) as the start of a piece, harmonize (b) as the conclusion:

(6) Add parts for S. A. T. above the following pedals without modulation:

(7) In separate examples, modulate on the following pedals as under:

(*a*) from B♭ major to C minor and back.
(*b*)   ,,   ,,   B♭ minor   ,,
(*c*)   ,,   ,,   E♭ major   ,,
(*d*)   ,,   ,,   F major   ,,
(*e*)   ,,   ,,   G minor   ,,

(β)
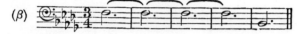

(*a*) from B♭ minor to E♭ minor and back.
(*b*)   ,,   ,,   F major   ,,

(γ)
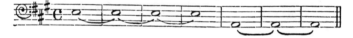

(*a*) from B♭ major to C minor and back.
(*b*)   ,,   .   E♭ minor   ,,
(*c*)   ,,   ,,   G minor   ,,

(8) On the dominant pedal in the following, modulate to B minor, F♯ minor and back, and on the tonic pedal to D minor and back :

(9) Add parts for S. and A. :

CHAPTER VII

ADDITIONAL EXERCISES

FOLLOWING the procedure at the end of Part II, this chapter gives additional exercises, including the resource discussed in Part III.

There are no new points to add, and the types of question are the same.

But the student should be warned against an undue use of chromaticism. No attempt should be made to drag in chromaticisms on every available occasion. They should only be introduced when their use seems appropriate and inevitable. Strong diatonic progressions should in the main predominate. A very sparing use should be made of diminished sevenths. In modulation they are apt to become the refuge of the destitute. Always examine the end of a melody or bass before working it, to make certain as to whether the key is major or relative minor. A melody that is in the minor key can be made to look as if it were in the relative major, and vice versa, and it is annoying to find when the working is nearly completed, that from want of foresight, the wrong key has been chosen, and that the problem must be re-worked. No problem should be attempted till the whole of the given part has been studied. And once having begun, nothing should be written without consideration of what has gone before and what is to come. Unless this is done, the student will be constantly forming entanglements for himself.

(1) Harmonize the following melodies for S. A. T. B. :

(a)

(2) Write in each of the following examples two phrases in four vocal parts (eight bars in all), introducing the chords given in any time value, and in any order (no modulation):

(3) The same, but with appropriate modulation in the second phrase, returning at the end to the tonic:

(4) Add parts for S. A. T.:

(5) Ground Basses:

(6) Modulations.

(*a*) Begin as follows, and modulate to D minor, **A major**,
D♭ major, and back to F :

(*b*) Begin as follows, and modulate to E minor, **B major**,
C major, and back to G :

(*c*) Begin as follows, and modulate to C minor, **B♭ major**,
G♭ major, E major, and back to E♭ :

(7) Add S. T. and B. to the following Alto parts :
(*a*)

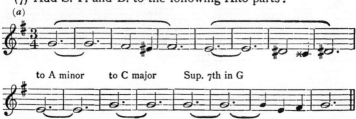

(8) Add S. A. B. to the following Tenor parts :

to F major   to Bb major

to C minor   to Eb major

CHAPTER VIII

ACCOMPANIMENT WRITING

1. A short theme for voice or violin is given. To this is to be added a simple accompaniment for the pianoforte.

2. **Pianoforte Writing.**

(*a*) Real parts are not required.

(*b*) The bass is often doubled in octaves in the left hand.

(*c*) Any *upper* parts may be doubled in octaves, but no upper part should move in consecutive octaves with the bass.

3. **Solo and Accompaniment.**

(*a*) The solo is not a real part. Any upper accompaniment part may move with it in octaves either momentarily or for some time. But the bass must not do so.

(*b*) The accompaniment should be complete in itself. If the leading note or a discord occur in the solo part, they *may* be doubled in the accompaniment.

Ex. 80.

(*c*) The accompaniment should not duplicate the solo part, except momentarily. It should confine itself to accompanying. The most that should be done is that the solo should be 'shadowed'.

Ex. 81.

VIOLIN.

PIANO.

4. Types of Accompaniment.

(a) Broken chords.

The following four-part passage:

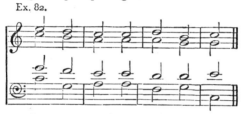

Ex. 82.

can be arranged as an arpeggio accompaniment, thus:

Ex. 83.

Note that the rests in the bass are merely ornamental. The note preceding the rest lasts in effect during the rests.

Various types of arpeggio, with or without unessential notes, can be devised on the above basis.

Ex. 84.

(b) Detached chords formed into rhythmic figures.

Ex. 85.

(*c*) Melodic figures, that is figures that are not merely rhythmic or arpeggio, but which contain some melodic interest.

Ex. 86.
One chord each bar.

In such cases care must be taken not to repeat the figure bar after bar. Rhythmic variety must be introduced, and relief should be given specially at the cadences.

Suppose the following to be the basis of the first four bars:

Ex. 87.

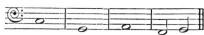

Bars three and four of the above examples would proceed somewhat thus:

Ex. 88.

And then the ear would stand a return to the original formula.

(*d*) A combination of (*b*) and short figures based on decorative resource (passing notes, auxiliary notes, &c.).

Ex. 89.

5. These types of accompaniment will serve for elementary work. All the types will not necessarily suit any one tune. Much depends upon the harmonic pattern of the tune. For example, if it demanded four chords in a bar the following would not do :

Ex 90.

If the figure chosen will fit most bars, but not all, it must be modified in the bars that will not stand it. And this variety is really a virtue.

Ex. 91.

In any case, even if the figure can be kept up rigidly, it is better to vary it, especially at the cadences.

Further, it is unnecessary to keep up one particular type of accompaniment throughout a stanza. Sometimes the beginning of the second half, or the middle requires a different figure, a return being made to the original one towards the end.

Or again, two figures may alternate:

Ex. 92.

then they may be used separately, and finally as in the original arrangement. The two cardinal points are that there must be unity and at the same time variety.

6. **The Introduction.** The accompaniment should have a few bars of introduction.

It should give out (*a*) the accompaniment figure, or (*b*) the opening phrase of the tune in addition to the accompaniment figure.

7. The Ending.   The following are usual means of ending:

(*a*) repetition of cadence chords with or without figure of accompaniment.

(*b*) a reference to some salient portion of the tune, generally either the opening or the end, accompanied with the figures used in the course of the setting.

Exercises.

(1) Add accompaniments for pianoforte to the following themes:

(1) Violin.

In each case start new figures at bar 9, and return to the original at bar 17.

(3) Add three varied accompaniments to each of the following:

(b) Voice.

(1)

(1) Treat G as an auxiliary note.

(c) Violin.

(d) Violin.

CHAPTER IX

SIMPLE VARIATIONS FOR PIANOFORTE

1. A simple theme, harmonized, is given.

The student is required to write elementary variants of this original version, in accordance with the instructions given in this chapter.

2. **Method I.** Decoration of the theme, by florid passages. This does not mean mere meandering by means of various sorts of unessential notes.

(*a*) When one particular kind of figure is kept up throughout, it is only tolerable if it contain no variety of rhythm, except possibly at the cadences.

Suppose the following to be the given theme:

Ex. 93.

It should be musically impossible for any one to think of a variation of the sort that follows:

Ex. 94.

It will be shown in due course what to do in such a case.

In the particular case under consideration, a uniform rhythm, variety must be obtained by variety of pattern, but according to some definite plan, which should be obvious from the formation of the theme.

It will be noted that the theme starts with two responsive phrases containing rhythmic variety. The variation should therefore have corresponding responsive phrases, with variety in curve.

The following is poor, because it leaves nothing to be done but start something else when it has become wearisome (but cf. p. 80):

Ex. 95.

This, however, is much better, because it contains two simple germinal ideas, auxiliary notes and arpeggio:

Ex. 96.

When this has been repeated once (bars 3 and 4) it is felt that development is a necessity.

The theme gives the cue. Bars 5 and 6 are shorter phrases, so we can shorten the figure by using the auxiliary notes pattern only.

Ex. 97.

The next two bars indicate and require change, but at the same time some uniformity.   So the left hand can be given the arpeggio figure, and finally the right hand returns to the auxiliary note figure for one bar, and the left hand takes the arpeggio for the next bar.   Thus we get uniformity together with variety.

Ex. 98 (1).

The example could also be worked in triple time, thus :

Ex. 98 (2).

The important thing then is to get at least two patterns of curve in a figure that is uniform in rhythm. And for a really successful use of this method the theme itself should have responsive phrases and development.

(*b*) The use of figuration containing rhythmic variety.

When a figure containing rhythmic variety is used, it should generally be of the same proportions as the phrase of the original.

It would be injudicious to use Ex. 94 as two statements of the figure occur over one phrase.

In considering what to use after

Ex. 99.

it would be well to think of what would be appropriate in bar 7, and introduce it in bar 2 (refer to Ex. 93).

Ex. 100.

The rest is plain sailing. Bars 3 and 4 will respond to bars 1 and 2. Bars 5 and 6 will use bar 1 only, and bars 7–8, bar 2, and the rest precisely as in the former example.

Ex. 101.

3. **Method II.** This consists of precisely the same principles, except that the ornamentation does *not* follow the curve of the tune. The harmonic basis is retained, but the figures do not 'dog' the tune.

In the following example the first part of the figure is imitated in the left hand in bars 2 and 4, then a section of it in bars 5 and 6 by inversion. In bar 8 the chord of the augmented sixth was discarded as being impracticable with a scale passage.

Ex. 102.

With this particular theme it would be possible to work a figure with only one rhythm and only one curve, without inducing monotony.   This is because the theme is itself constructed so as to give variety both harmonically and rhythmically sufficient to prevent this fault.   The sub-phrases of bars 5 and 6, and the extension of the last phrase are the factors of this result.

Ex. 103.

But a tune with the harmony marching uniformly all the way, and with the phrases all the same, would not stand such treatment.

If such a bad theme as the following were set for variations:

Ex. 104.

its grave faults would have to be minimized in the variations. In elementary work, we are not considering alteration of proportions, all we can do is to relieve the monotony of the rhythm.

Ex. 105.

In the above at (a) and (b) will be observed minor deviations from the original harmony. This a common device.

4. **Method III.** Change of mode, from major to minor, or

vice versa, with necessary deviations from the corresponding
harmony.

Ex. 106.

5. **Method IV.**   Utilizing the principles mentioned we can
use different keys, provided the keys follow on in some logical
way.   And we can change the time-signature.   For example,
figures could be worked on the harmonic basis turned into triple
time.

Ex. 107.   Cf. Ex. 98 (2).

6. **Method V.**   The theme may be retained, but harmonized
differently, and accompanied in a different way from that in the
original.   This treatment depends upon the harmonic possibilities of the theme.   The theme under consideration could
go into G minor in bars 3 and 4, E♭ major in bar 5, and C minor
in bar 6.

Ex. 108.

7. Method VI. If the theme contain a fair amount of rhythmic variety, and ideas that can be detached, some of these can be used as figures for separate variations, and developed on the harmonic basis of the theme.

Ex. 109.

Here in the first four bars are three ideas that could be used:

Ex. 110.

8. There are, of course, several other methods.   But these
will suffice for elementary work.   The examples written do not
pretend to any value as composition.   It was thought better to
write examples of this sort rather than quote classics, so that the
student might see that all that is required at present is some
facility and technique.   Any average student ought to be able
to write such examples as have been given in this chapter at

any hour in the day, and to an unlimited extent.   If such work does nothing else, it gives practice in the use of figuration, and affords relief from other types of problems, besides calling forth a certain amount of ingenuity and musical gumption.

(1) Write a few variations on each of the following:

(1)

(2)

(3)

Notes on the Exercises.

(1) 1st phrase, bars 1–2.

    2nd   ,,   responsive bars 3–4 (get variety at the cadence).

    Sub-phrases, bars 5 and 6 (new material).

    Last phrase, bars 7–10; extended by sequence (bar 8) and cadential extension, referring to the opening phrase.

This formation should be reproduced with variations, by using the figures in a corresponding manner.

(2) 1st phrase, bars 1–2.

    2nd ,,   ,,   3–4, contrasted.

    3rd ,,   ,,   5–6 (repetition of first part of 1st phrase).

    4th ,,   ,,   7–8 (corresponding to 2nd phrase).

(3) 1st phrase, bars 1–2; the first half divisible into two figures, the second half being one section.

    2nd phrase, bars 3–5; extended by one bar, first half divisible into two figures, second half extended by prolonging the chord (a). The normal form can be seen by omitting bar 4.

(4) 1st phrase, bars 1–2; divided into two sections (corresponding).

    2nd phrase, bars 3–4 (not divisible into sections).

    3rd ,,   ,,   5–6; same formation as 1st phrase.

    4th ,,   ,,   7–9; same as 2nd phrase, with extension caused by lengthening the cadence chords.

(5) 1st phrase, bar 1.

    2nd ,,   ,,   2; responsive.

    3rd ,,   ,,   3–4; contrasted, and extended by imitation.

    4th ,,   ,,   5–6 (cf. 1st phrase).

(Or, 1st phrase, bars 1–2; containing two responsive sections.

    2nd ,,   ,,   3–4; contrasted.

    3rd ,,   ,,   5–6; referring to 1st phrase, but not divisible.)

(6) Two responsive phrases of two bars each. (The accompaniment forms a canon at the octave at a quaver's distance.)

All these several formations should be reproduced in the new figurations.

APPENDIX

PART I, CHAPTER XI

Add:

Suppose a melody in the minor key contained the following progression:

Key A minor.

and it be intended to avoid modulation, the G♮ must be treated as an accented passing note:

For

    (*a*) it is inartistic to harmonize both G and F, as they are notes of short duration;

    (*b*) G♮ is only used as a harmony note to reach F♮, a harmony note. If, therefore, G were the harmony note, and F the passing note, there would be no reason for substituting G♮ for G♯.

If the progression occurred after the first phrase, and if modulation were available, the following would be correct:

Modulation to C major.

It is not to be inferred from this that the following is incorrect:

But it must be understood that it is modal harmony (see *Evolution of Harmony*, Chap. II), and not a proper harmonization of the minor scale.

PART II, CHAPTER V

KEYS that are nearly related to one particular key have not necessarily this relation to one another. For example, both G major and F major are nearly related to C major, but G major and F major have not this relationship.

In this chapter the cycle of keys to which modulations are made is confined to those nearly related to the tonic. But in the course of the cycle, though consecutive keys may not be nearly related to one another, no new principles of modulation are involved.

INDEX

References to Part II have (2) placed after their page numbers.

    ,,   ,,   III   ,,   (3)   ,,   ,,   ,,   ,,